ADRIFT ON A SEA
OF BLUE LIGHT

Pete T. Milerly

BREATH
ST. JOHN, U.S.V.I.

To my parents, John and Virginia Muilenburg,
Who have run the good race
And won.

This collection contains true stories, most of which were originally published in *SAIL, Reader's Digest, Islands* and elsewhere.

SAIL first published
Methuselah Meets Hotspur
Tropical Weather Outlook
Boobies and the Mystic
Saga of a Seagoing Dog
Santos and the Elephant
Old Luke
Sombrero
Passage to Palermo
Navigating Dog
On Shipwrecks and Sailors
Face to Face at Ocean Bight (Crossroads at Inagua)

Islands first published
Joy and Grief on the Las Aves Reef
Azores High (In Search of a Warm Vent)
The Parrot
Lignum Vitae
Another Island . . . Another Library
Beat the Bank
A Lighthouse to Love
The House
Dreaming Treasure

Reader's Digest published
Saga of a Seagoing Dog
Boobies and the Mystic
Destiny at Denton Bridge (A Dog Like No Other)

American Way published
Galvanized in Paradise

Guideposts published
The Tire Iron

Contents

Acknowledgements

Thanks to Amy Ullrich, managing editor at *SAIL* who encouraged (and bought) my first pieces, for her advice and friendship over the years. Also to James Badham, formerly of *Islands*, who gave me a column on the Caribbean to write; and to Brian Summers once of *Reader's Digest*, another good friend and editor.

Heartfelt appreciation to my extraordinary neighbors, Pat and Emily Cena for all they have done in aid of this project.

I want to thank the Archivos General de las Indias in Seville, for the four months I was privileged to do research there.

Gracias amigo to Don E. Brown, editor, counselor, kindred spirit.

Finally, eclipsing all others, I thank my dear wife, Dorothy, for her faith and her patience, all these years.

Way back in 1968, a young couple with hippie tendencies arrived, fresh from college and the tumult of the times, at the little West Indian Island of St. John. They lived on the beach and when their money ran out they got teaching jobs and bought a boat to live on, and in doing so cast themselves onto the currents of the great oceanic drift that bathes the West Indies and circles the North Atlantic.

She was a gifted teacher, and if she'd had her way would have stayed at her school on St. John. But her husband wanted to sail, and he carried her away on their boat, first a 28-foot sloop in which they crisscrossed the Caribbean, then in the 42-foot gaff-rigged ketch he built on a St. John beach.

In that boat, Breath, they made two round trip voyages to the Mediterranean and West Africa, as well as numerous voyages between North and South America. One doesn't put that many miles under the keel without some remarkable encounters and close calls.

These became the captain's yarns, which he first told to his charter guests back on St. John, then published in various magazines. The locales range from a cold mountaintop in the Azores to the cactus flats on Bonaire; from the muddy delta of the Gambia River to the transparent waters of the Las Aves reef. These are sea stories, filled with a feel for St. John, the West Indies, and the wondrous sea in which they are set.

Hurricane, shipwreck and treasure lie within these pages, as do smugglers, snorkelers, drunks, donkeys, a feisty little sea-going dog, a Holocaust survivor, a kleptomaniac cat, turtles in trouble, a sailor searching out past lives, a family seeking the admiral's silver, a father praying for his son to make it through the night, and much more.

While each chapter can be read independently, the tales are arranged in chronological order and form a narrative of a way of life spent upon the great North Atlantic drift — adrift but not without direction.

— P. M.

ADRIFT ON A SEA OF BLUE LIGHT

1.

THE BOOBIES AND THE MYSTIC

My younger son, Diego, still wonders if some mystical force didn't raise that storm to send us searching for shelter in those remote islands. Otherwise, we wouldn't have stopped there and the birds might be dying yet. Well — mystical, maybe. As Hamlet said, there are more things in heaven and earth than are dreamt of in our philosophies. Still, I figure it was a coincidence.

Dawn on a late August morning found us 100 miles north of the Venezuelan mainland. The night had grown calm, and haze obscured the stars, tainting the early light with a dull, uneasy yellow. I watched with growing concern. At midnight the U.S. Coast Guard had announced the formation of a rapidly intensifying tropical depression that might become a storm within 24 hours. If the forecast was right, we'd be experiencing the onset of bad weather by evening.

Our summer charter season on St. John in the U.S. Virgin Islands had ended, and the autumn hurricane season had begun, so we were moving our 42-foot ketch, Breath, down to the safety of the lower latitudes. We had waited for good weather and set sail on the heels of a tropical wave. That gave us about three good days to get safely south before the next wave, with its storm-spawning potential, moved into the Caribbean. We had just made it into Venezuela's territorial waters that morning as we closed with the long string of islands and reefs that parallel its coast 80 miles offshore. Theoretically, we had won. Depressions aren't supposed to form that far south. Nonetheless, this one was heading straight for us like a bullet with our name on it.

Nearby lay the desolate Islas de Las Aves de Barlovento, a 5-mile long, semicircular barrier reef that shelters a lagoon of shallows, reefs, and uninhabited cays. Somewhere within that maze of coral and mangrove we hoped to find a sheltered spot where we could safely ride out bad weather.

The problem was determining exactly where these islands were. My DR plot put us 10 or 15 miles away, but the uncertain currents could have deposited us anywhere in a 35-mile swath. Overcast skies precluded new sights and I had no electronic substitute for the sextant.

The islands are so low that we'd have to be on top of them to see them, but I sent my two sons up the ratlines periodically for a look. As we drew near, another undulating line appeared in the distance and behind them yet another. Wave after wave of boobies out of the south-southeast. Islas de las Aves — Islands of the Birds — it didn't take a Polynesian sorcerer to make the connection.

We pointed our bow toward the center of the birds, and within 90 minutes the first smudges of land appeared on the horizon. They steadily merged to become a line of mangroves behind a white ribbon of breaking reef. Soon Breath was rolling in the steepened rebound just outside. Then we passed into the flat water of the lee, dropped the hook behind the largest cay and lay at ease.

Directly to windward grew a forest wall of ancient mangroves, the grandest we'd ever seen, whose gnarled trunks rose majestically above the tangle of the sturdy roots. The trees were alive with boobies. Their flight filled the air as did their mewing, croaking calls our ears, while the wild reek of guano and swamp overwhelmed our nostrils. We saw what a multitude they were soon after our arrival, when a squall enveloped the lagoon. A single stroke of lightning flicked like a livid switchblade out of the overhanging darkness, instantly followed by a crack of thunder. Every bird in the forest pelted up from its roost in blind panic, flapping and groaning; their numbers dimmed the light still more.

We felt their fear and looked at our anchorage, which was wide open to the west. The bottom felt like patchy sand over loose coral, and big heads broke the surface not far from the boat. If we got a blow from the west at night, we'd be dragging through a minefield of breaking heads in the dark. We had to find something better or leave.

We set out in the dinghy, exploring and sounding with the lead, until eventually we found a channel that wound its way past the reefs and shallows into a limpid pool of deep water. By mid-afternoon we had brought Breath into it where she rode placidly to her biggest anchors. Here she was completely surrounded by mangroves, breaking reefs and drying sandbanks. Beyond the latter, the long barrier reef stopped the swell, murmuring at its work. In such a spot we could defy all but the worst weather.

Diego had a strong attachment to our small green parrot, which has sparked an interest in birds generally. So with nothing to do now but wait, he and I decided to explore the mangroves for a closer look at the boobies. We paddled the dinghy to shore, slipped under the overhanging branches, and balanced barefoot on the springy roots in the cool, mute shadows.

Every tree held nesting boobies. We could approach them to within an arm's length if we moved slowly. Considerably less pleased by the encounter than we, they watched us with baleful, nervous stares. If we got too close, they pecked, not at us, but at the air or a branch to show how fearsome they were. Yet if we persisted, they would thrash reluctantly out of the foliage and soar about anxiously until we withdrew.

For years I had admired the boobies' clean, strong lines, their immaculate, blade-like wings, and the rich chocolate and pristine white of their feathers. Never had I imagined that up close, their beaks and eyes would be so delicately traced with soft iridescent lavender and turquoise. Their young, innocent and demure in pure white baby fluff, looked like tufts of fair-weather cumulus that had wafted too low and become lodged in a magic forest.

© Don E. Brown 2004

As we were most charmed and lulled by that gentle nursery, our gaze was assaulted by an ugly sight — a booby, dead, caught by a wing tip in the foliage. Its other wing stretched toward earth, and a caravan of ants streamed out of its eye sockets. It was like seeing a gibbet.

We stepped into a small clearing and there in thin air, two more boobies dangled dead, each caught by a wing. One was desiccated, its feathers falling out, but the other was newly dead, its plumage still bright and plump. The hairs stood up on the back of my neck. I muttered a sailor's oath. Diego stood riveted, eyes wide. The swamp oozed a sudden malevolence. Then a gust of wind swayed the bodies and a shaft of light flashed on the culprit — an almost invisible length of 20-pound-test nylon fishing line stretched over the treetops.

We began following the thin blue filament, over and through the mangroves, and finally found its terminus, a rusty old hook embedded in a bleached booby skull, high in the crotch of a tree. We counted nine more hanging corpses, each caught the same way — the line tightly crimped around the quills of strong flight feathers. On the ground beneath lay the remains of yet earlier victims — clumps of feathers, scattered bones, a beak and skull. We tore the line down, cut it to shreds, and buried it with the corpses under a pile of brush.

A vivid sequence clicked into place. The original victim must have snatched up a fisherman's trolled bait, very likely a fresh ballahou artfully rigged to make it skim, lifelike, just below the surface. When he saw the bird's frantic struggles, the fisherman must have taken pity on the creature, given up some 100 meters of line, and cut the booby free to work out the hook as best it might — a well-meant mistake. Off flew the bird, headed for home, trailing the long, invisible, snarly, impervious synthetic line.

How much better had the booby entangled its own wings and fallen bound into the sea! Once it reached the mangroves of Las Aves, its tribe was cursed. Flying in and out of their nests, a percentage of them caught their wings and were hung in torment until the sun and wind parched their lives away. That line might have remained there for years to come, taking a steady toll. The birds hadn't learned to avoid it and never would. The expression "birdbrain" came forcefully to mind. Not for nothing had the Spaniards who explored this region called the booby "bobo" or "simpleton" in Castilian. Still, we grieved for them and thought about the consequences of man-made intrusions into the world of nature. Filled with the experience, we headed back to the boat. The weather was suddenly much improved. Blue expanded rapidly in the sky, and the remaining overcast was breaking up into smaller clumps. A light but steady breeze filled in. We tuned in the evening weather broadcast, and of all the luck, the depression had stalled. Instead of intensifying, it was dissipating.

"So, what are you thinking, kid?" I asked Diego, who was uncharacteristically quiet, absorbed in the fiery red clouds on the horizon. Shafts of pink and blue radiated up from the sunken sun. All around us in the anchorage flew thousands of boobies and terns.

"Ah, you'll just laugh at me," he shrugged.

"Whaddya mean? I swear I won't! Come on, tell me."

"Well, they're thanking us," he said gravely.

"What?"

"The birds. They're thanking us. Can you feel it? Look, they're all out there flying a sort of dance."

There did seem to be a pattern in their flight, a large figure eight that glided low over the water and up and around the mangroves.

"And that storm," he added.

"Yeah?"

"Well, do you think it was...normal...for it to just disappear? Right after we cut that line down? It seems like..."

Silence. I waited.

"Maybe they were leading us to this place all along. Something was going on."

How do you answer a 10-year-old mystic?

2.

SAGA OF A SEAGOING DOG

Our little captain was lost at sea. We'd last seen him precariously balanced between the bowsprit and the knighthead, eagerly sniffing at the mountains appearing on the dawn horizon. He who barked furiously at the hint of danger to others made not a whimper when he slipped and fell overboard five miles off the Venezuelan coast.

We didn't miss him until we had anchored our 42-foot ketch, Breath, behind a breakwater at the foot of the coastal sierras, after a rolly overnight passage from the offshore islands. Suddenly, our son Diego called out in alarm, "Hey, where's Santos?"

We searched everywhere. Diego tore open our last bag of Doritos, noisily crackling the plastic and calling the dog, but he was long gone. My wife and I went ashore to notify Puerto Azul's port captain that an exhausted small dog might appear on the premises. Although busy with the start of a sport-fishing tournament, he promised to keep an eye out. He offered us the facilities of the club, so we sat at the lighthouse bar and thought about what to tell our son.

Santos had been such a wonderful character. Brave and loving, irrepressible and reckless. Time and again we had feared for his life. He'd been hit by cars, nearly drowned, held for ransom. An endlessly amusing, extremely handsome little rogue, he was Diego's constant companion and a useful member of the crew.

Well, easy come, easy go. He'd been given to us in the first place. Years ago, in a Florida port, we'd anchored next to a 26-foot sloop with two people and 7 dogs on board. Jean and Vince were raising schipperkes, the Dutch boat dogs, and five puppies had recently been born. We didn't have the money for a pedigreed dog, but on the day we left, Jean came over and offered our two sons the pick of the litter, free. "Your ship needs a schipperke," she declared.

Privately, I didn't think so. I was still building the interior and didn't need a leaky puppy in the sawdust. But my objections blew away in a williwaw of enthusiasm from the crew. So I reminded the boys, as they rowed over, to "pick a lively one," traditional wisdom handed down from my father. How little I knew about schipps! They returned with a ball of jet-black fluff that sat in my palm, looked me dead in the eye, and growled.

Before he was three months old, he'd almost drowned twice. Charging down the deck in a puppy war game, he shot right out a scupper, he was so tiny. We heard a scratching sound on the hull and went topside to find baby Santos treading cold water and scrabbling with his forepaws at the boot-top. Luckily, it was slack tide; half an hour later he would have been riding a 4-knot current out the Port Canaveral inlet. A month later, in the Exumas, he did it again, and the ebb tide carried him out the cut while we were below at lunch. A returning skin-diver noticed his black head with pointed ears and picked him up.

He was an unusual beast. Our friend Greg Rochlin called him "a hamster masquerading as a wolf," but on closer inspection he looked like a cross between a fox and a husky, pint size.

In time, he developed into a fine boat dog. He learned to stay out of the way and to keep his footing in heavy seas. He never got seasick or knocked over the coffee or varnish, and he maintained such a stoical lock on his bladder that he would groan with anticipation as the dinghy finally neared the shore. People loved to see his shaggy head fill a porthole, like a trophy mounted in the galley, where he could follow the cook's every move with a devoted eye. And he was endearing company, especially on long night watches when he would creep unbidden into the lonely helmsman's lap and rest his muzzle with a sigh of contentment in one's hand.

A salty dog, but only a fair-weather sailor. Lying in the shade of a sail, watching the land go by, sampling the scents of shore — this he enjoyed; but going to windward in anything over Force 4 he loathed. At the first drops of spray, he would scurry to the companionway and beg to be taken below. Rough weather made it difficult to use the old coil of rope on the foredeck that served as his high seas privy. Unfortunately, this also made us reluctant to have him below, circling restlessly in some dark corner. So up in the cockpit he huddled, constipated, his eyes red with salt, flinching every time the bow thumped a wave. Not surprisingly, when he noticed the dinghy go up on deck, he grew visibly depressed.

Intelligence in such a dog can be a two-edged sword. He well knew what was expected of him, but he also had his own agenda of fun and this got him into trouble regularly. In Puerto Cabello, Venezuela, he jumped ship to join a weekend throng of people and dogs partying at a nearby beach and didn't come home. We searched the town without result, and by the next night opinion on the dock had him "perro caliente" at a waterfront restaurant. Our sons grew frantic. "Dad, we've got to do something!"

So, I went to the local radio station and broadcast a reward — only $15, but in gritty Puerto Cabello that would ransom a child. I could see the dollar signs glinting in the hard eyes of the station manager's girlfriend. She got hold of the dog, but refused to hand him over except for double the reward. Dorothy played "American," rich and dumb, ready to pay whatever to get her dear doggie back — but she didn't have the money on her — she'd send her husband with it right away. They finally gave her the dog, she sent me, I refused to give them another dime and the extortion attempt fizzled without rancor; they were just trying their luck.

Schipperke means "little captain" in Flemish so it was no coincidence that Santos adapted so well to life afloat. His ancestors were bred centuries ago to serve aboard Low Country barges. They had to be small, useful as watchdogs and ratters, and waterproof. Their duties included swimming ashore in the cold canals to nip the heels of recalcitrant tow horses. Genetically programmed to raise a storm of barking the instant anyone fell overboard, the dogs made ideal babysitters for the family-run vessels. They were even credited with helping the master navigate. Dead-reckoning dogs? Santos made me think twice.

One night we were beating to windward in Force 6 and rain, trying to gain the shelter of Mayaguana in the far-out Bahamas. After 36 hours of overcast, we couldn't be sure of our position. Suddenly, Santos roused himself from sodden misery and stood with his nose straining into the wind. He whimpered ardently. What could it be but the scent of land borne on the wind? We turned on the engine and short-tacked up the olfactory bearing, and within two hours we picked up the light.

Everything that worked for the Dutch barges works for a cruising boat today. Schipperkes definitely discourage rats and intruders. In Seville, a city notorious for ingenious thieves, Santos's paranoid mistrust of strangers made him popular among those at the dock with something to lose. When I apologized for his barking, people often replied, "He's just doing his job."

His water-resistant coat dried with three good shakes and a few minutes in the sun — no boat needs a wet dog. His instinctive barking when people "fell in" could be a nuisance when friends were diving off the rail, yet the trait might someday save a child's life; and during bumpy night watches, when he was the only one on deck with the helmsman, we thought of him as a man-overboard alarm.

It was time to get back to Diego; we couldn't postpone the inevitable any longer.

"Oh well," I consoled Dorothy, "with his temperament we were lucky to have him as long as we did." She nodded.

"And now we won't have to always be cleaning up after him." Schipperkes shed a lot and are sloppy; we used to find bits of food, and occasional "mistakes" on the deck.

Still silent.

"And no more hair-trigger barking," I continued. He'd made us enemies more than once, usually alcoholics in nearby slips whose late-morning hangovers his shrill bark penetrated like a hot poker.

Dorothy's eyes brimmed. "I just keep remembering the good things — how he took food from my fingers so gently, and always thanked me. He was such a dear little dog. To think of him out there all alone!" A tear started down her cheek.

What could I say? I paid for the drinks and we walked to the dinghy. I was casting off when we heard a shout. The port captain came hurrying down the steps from his office with a big grin on his face.

"You won't believe it. I was just calling the boats on the radio to tally their midday standings for the scoreboard..." He paused, out of breath.

"And?" We gasped.

"And the last boat said they caught nothing — except a little black dog!"

There couldn't be two of them swimming around out there.

We were at the dock when the Nena II pulled in. True to Latin style, the whole family was on board, infant to grandmother, including the maid. The captain's mother had spotted Santos about five miles out, rising and falling on the swell, as the boat sped out to the favored fishing grounds. She insisted that her son turn the boat around to take a closer look, marlin or no marlin. They scooped him out with a hand net and by the end of the day were sorry to part with him.

Back on Breath he received a joyous welcome and got his very own helping of the family dinner, but his eyes were glazed, as if they'd seen the whole of his life pass before them in the hour of swimming with his death. Right after supper he crashed. When I drifted off later, I thought about what a charmed life he led and that maybe the experience would make a more sensible animal of him.

That fantasy died at dawn, when a flurry of barking awoke us. A fisherman had dared to pass within 150 feet of our boat. A few hours later, seeing some kids playing with a German shepherd on the beach, Santos jumped into the dinghy, then into the sea and headed for the action. The first we heard of it was when someone knocked on the hull.

"Hello, is this your dog? We found him swimming past our boat."

Yup. That's our dog.

3.

THE HOUSE

Late one afternoon in hurricane season, way back in the 30's, a schooner ghosted into a quiet cove on St. John and dropped anchor. The rattle of its chain caught the attention of a boy in the hills collecting soldier crabs for bait. Looking out, he saw three white men lining the rail and staring hungrily at the land, like they had been a long time at sea.

Early next morning they came ashore and, when they could find someone to talk to, announced they were looking for land to buy — in Chocolate Hole, the same cove where they were anchored. This was most unusual. It was the depths of the depression; people were leaving the Virgin Islands to seek employment in Curacao, New York, or Santo Domingo. Land was almost worthless — you could buy an acre for the price of a cow.

St. John was a remote backwater back then — population of 700, no electricity, no roads to speak of, the only vehicles horse and cart. Most people traveled by sailboat and lived close to the sea in settlements on the east side with names like John's Folly, Hard Labor and Palestina.

No one lived in Chocolate Hole. Located at the SW corner of the island, its only virtue lay in being easy for a vessel to enter under sail, which also meant it was dangerous in south winds. Additionally it was in the rain shadow, thus hot, arid, sorely molested with mosquitoes and sandflies, and covered with vicious thorny scrub.

After days of doggedly hiking up and down the hills in the briars and the blistering heat, they chose a lot that couldn't have been worse, close to the boy's best spot for soldier crabs, in the lee of a prominent boulder, that would be hot and buggy even by Chocolate Hole standards. They refused to be dissuaded. They said they loved the view that conveniently looked down on their boat in the cove below.

Well, white people were already known to buy a piece of land — be it ever so steep, rocky, and exposed — solely because it had a great view. The owner pocketed the cash without further demurral and the deal was done.

The newcomers didn't waste much time. They took the schooner to Charlotte Amalie and returned with a load of lumber. They hired a carpenter, the boy's uncle, who lived in Cruz Bay, and began framing a house, the white men working hard alongside, with scarcely a break even at noon. They laid out a good-sized house, but didn't bother with cement foundations or a concrete cistern. Instead they built it on posts of lignum vitae and brought a couple of barrels ashore from the schooner for their water supply — both were commonly used for small shingle-sided cabins, but not for a proper house of this size. The carpenter shook his head

As the days passed the house went up quickly, but the carpenter grew ever more displeased. Island carpenters in those days built boats as well as houses, and they built both to last. But not this house. The continentals, despite his advice, his warnings about hurricanes, were using the cheapest lumber and tacking it together with nails.

At the end of each week's work the carpenter would hold forth at the rum shop in Cruz Bay on the latest eccentricities of his employment. The house had no first floor windows — the white men said they would put them in later! Then the floor — instead of hardwood, cheap pine! Already it was splintering. And the roof beams — merely toe-nailed instead of the traditional, carefully fitted mortise and tenon joints! The carpenter predicted the first good blow would take it all away. The men nodded and fired back shots of white rum while the boys listened outside.

The walls and roof erected, the continentals declared they would finish the interior themselves. That was just fine with the carpenter who washed his hands of the project and resumed working on a fishing boat he was building, properly, on the beach in Cruz Bay.

A month went by during which there was little apparent progress on the house, though lights burned late into the night. The men were invariably polite, but kept to themselves. They met visitors at a distance from the house; nobody was ever invited in, not even the administrator when he stopped by one sweltering afternoon — and he was a white man like them. When the boy came near the property to search for soldier crabs he was shooed off without ceremony.

Even for continentals they seemed obsessed with privacy — but what did three men need such privacy for? It didn't bear thinking on!

Then, one morning the schooner was gone and the house deserted. Days passed, the boat didn't return, and the boy felt emboldened to check his favorite spot for crabs, near the back of the house. Nobody came out to chase him away. He told his uncle but the carpenter enjoined him and the other boys to stay away from property that wasn't theirs.

The schooner had been gone a week when a night of terrible weather brought fearful strokes of lightning, heavy rains and high winds to the island. In the morning the boy, passing by, noticed that the door was open, banging in the wind, so he went to shut it. He took a look inside and went running for his uncle. Before long a knot of dumfounded people stood looking into the house.

The interior was piled with high with dirt. Hillocks of loose earth reached almost to the ceiling. The cheap pine floor was completely ripped up and now braced up the heaps, in between which gaped several deep holes. A wheelbarrow and some work worn picks and shovels leaned against a wall. A stout eyebolt in the roof's ridge beam held a block and tackle which suspended a large metal bucket over one of the holes. At the bottom of the biggest hole was a smaller one.

It didn't take anybody more than five seconds to figure out what the continentals had been digging for.

The Spanish conquistadors had ransacked two continents for gold, sending a prodigious river of wealth from the New World to Spain. A rivulet of it had been diverted — by pirates and hurricanes — into the Caribbean, of which a tiny trickle had ended up buried in the Virgin Islands. Fate was fluid for those who lived by canvas and cutlass and many never lived to withdraw the deposit they had banked in the discrete earth. It's still there today, if only one knew where to look.

How had the continentals known where to dig? A map? A family tradition that some adventurous descendant finally put to the test? Whatever, it had brought three men and a schooner all the way down from...where? No one knew just where they had come from and no one knew to where they had disappeared. So the white people weren't so crazy after all! Or were they? Did they actually find the treasure? Did the schooner survive the storm? No one ever knew.

Soon all traces of the episode were gone. The house blew away in a gale of wind, and heavy downpours filled in much of the holes and caved in the sides.

It seems all traces of the story are gone too. Nobody I asked about it — old natives and long time residents alike — remembered hearing about it. I heard it from an old fisherman, long since dead, who mended his nets on the beach where I landed my dinghy. He was a fount of information about the island and the sea. I'd bring a cold beer or two and he'd talk.

His story — he was the young boy getting soldier crabs — has stuck in my mind for 30 years. To me it has the hard-edged ring of truth, like a gold coin tossed onto the counter of a Port Royal saloon...

It must be true.

4

DREAMING TREASURE

Caves had never been my thing. I realized that now. But here we were, high up a rainy mountain in Dominica — and there it was, a dark hole in the hillside. Rain dripped down steadily from the top of the hole, like a little waterfall over the entrance.

"You want to go in first, Mr. G?" I suggested.

"Fust? No suh! Not last neither — me ain' goin' atall!"

I had engineered this — I couldn't just walk away now. I knelt in the mud and peered into the hole. My flashlight played on the walls of a short, narrow tunnel that opened up after five feet into a chamber — where something gleamed a dull white... silvery! My God, could it really be? Adrenalin in my throat, I wriggled forward. The flashlight went out — but I kept going.

It all started at Seville, in the archives, when one of the professional researchers handed me a list of documents. "You'll find these interesting. They're about treasure!"

The Archivos General de las Indias, repository of Spanish colonial documents, had provided crucial clues to the wreck of the Atocha, a fabulous treasure, and the venerable institution hadn't quite recovered from treasure fever. No one believed I had really come there to research 16th century Afro-Carib resistance in the Caribbean. They figured it was a cover for treasure prospecting ...after all, I owned an ocean-going boat, lived in the West Indies — hey, they weren't born yesterday.

The Carib Indians were still lords of the Lesser Antilles well into the 1600's, fierce warriors who voyaged throughout the eastern Caribbean in enormous dugouts in search of booty — the "shake yo booty" kind. Besides abducting attractive women they also assaulted Spanish shipping and settlements. Carib and Spaniard hated each other on sight like two fighting cocks. They deserved each other.

The documents were letters (circa 1588) from the governor of Puerto Rico who had just heard the testimony of Luisa Navarrete, a mulatta in her thirties who was married to a Spaniard and was by all accounts "a worthy Christian woman." Ten years previously she had been carried off, along with a number of enslaved Africans, to Dominica, stronghold of the Carib islands.

In her four years of captivity she learned the language, got friendly with her captors and found out about a Spanish ship carrying bullion that had wrecked at Dominica. The gold and silver from that ship and the loot gathered in almost a century of raids had been piled up in a cave for safekeeping. She had seen it and could find it again.

That letter bridged 400 years, and fired my imagination. In effect, I had a treasure map — if a little vague — to riches that were probably gone. However... anything might have happened since 1588 — hurricane, earthquake, pestilence, warfare. The only thing I knew for sure was that the next time I stopped at Dominica I'd definitely check out a cave or two.

I barely got the anchor down in Portsmouth Bay before young men on shore took to the water like crocodiles falling off a mud bank; a flotilla of small craft started splashing my way. A dinghy leaping at each oar stroke, hotly pursued by a paddler on a surfboard, arrived first. An uproar of laughter and repartee ensued.

"Mistah, you gon' buy yo banana from I!" the rower shouted to me.

"Nah, nah, I wa heah fuss! I de mon he gon' deal wid!" countered the paddler.

"Oh gahhh…he could lie? Wha' you mean 'fuss!' Me waitin' on you long time na!"

"Yo untrut' self!"

"Git from heah!"

A youth in a tiny dugout couldn't get past the bigger fellows. I liked his looks. "Hey you! In the dugout! Can you get sweet grapefruit?"

"Yeah boss! Sweetes' grapefruit in Dominica! Stan' back, I comin' through!" He crowed triumphantly.

Galahad — universally known as "Mr. G" — was 17, bright, and whatever we needed, he had a relative who could supply it. I got to like him and wondered if he could come up with a likely treasure cave.

"I don't expect to find treasure…. but you never know… an old sword, any trace, would be a thrill."

He thought about it for a while, and then said:

"Skip…. I got a aunty, she live by herself on top a mountain — she know a lot. People come to she to… fin' out t'ings."

"What kind of things?"

"Oh, you know…t'ings. Wha' could help dere life. And she know bush tea, could cure people. She old…wise…"

"How old?"

"Ah ain' t'ink even she own self know…old, old…"

"Maybe she can help us find the cave."

"Dass a good idea, skip."

"Can I bring her something…. a present?"

"Pipe tobacco," he answered, then added:

"An' she blind."

Mr. G's aunt was aged to perfection. The years seemed to have burnished away all dross, leaving only enough to see her by. A tight halo of wispy silvered curls clung about her head. Her wrinkled skin, intricately etched year-by-year, resembled flat calm water ruffled by a sudden breeze. Her hands, almost translucent, quivered slightly like feathers above the beat of a bird's heart.

" 'Drum'… bon tabac. Merci." she said, smelling it. Sensing more than touching, her fingers found a pipe on a shelf. Then she sat down in her rocking chair, a beautiful piece of work, handmade from local hardwoods, each joint whittled to fit and lashed prettily with strips of cane. Puffing daintily on her pipe, she listened to Mr. G's recital of family news, and of our quest, then, after a period of reflection she spoke, very slowly, as if she were in a trance. Mr. G translated in a whisper.

"There was a treasure long ago, kept in a cave and perhaps some still remains... but nobody can tell you where to find it. Only the spirits know, and if you are the one, they send you a dream. You must dream treasure... dream treasure! But...if you get a dream you must follow it — exactly — or else when you find a chest and open it — out come angry black stinging ants!"

Presently she got up and went outside her kitchen door and into her garden. She brushed through the plants, grasping their leaves gently, moving from one plant to another with familiar ease, and they brushed back, glad of her touch. She picked some leaves and gave them to me.

"Make bush tea and drink before you sleep," said Mr. G.

I had a wild, whirling night of dreams. All I remembered was trying to hide behind a waterfall, but losing my footing and starting to fall. When I woke I decided to drive around, find a cave and go for it, dream or no dream. It was time.

Mr. G and I drove over the spine of the island to Salybia, the Carib Indian reservation where a remnant of the Carib nation still lives and pursues their ancient culture. It seemed an appropriate place to start our quest in the absence of any more specific clue. From a man whose features might have passed for Mongolian we received lengthy instructions in patois that eventually turned Mr. G's confident look into a frown of concentration, then into something more dubious. What confidence we set off with we soon lost as the rental car shuddered up worse and worse roads, deeper into the rugged, cloud enshrouded hills.

By mid-afternoon, after several false starts, we finally found a local informant — Lorenzo, the leader of a gang of bright-eyed urchins playing kickball on the road. He was an amusing little loudmouth, bold as brass, caked in mud, dressed in a ragged

Chicago Bulls T-shirt. His oversized shorts flopped as he walked. But he swore he knew a cave, which he'd show us for a dollar.

After a half hour's tramping up the rainy mountain on a muddy track no better than a goat trail, I was ready to quit; but Lorenzo kept up a manic patter, pointing out birds, flowers, and every other minute claiming we were almost there. Finally he came to a halt and stuck out his hand.

"Lajon pwemiere!" he said in patois to Mr. G. Even I understood that — "money first." Mr. G raised a fist and Lorenzo, with a cry of triumph, started pulling aside ferns and elephant ears — revealing a hole in the hillside.

I fished out a damp buck and asked him, "You ever been inside?"

"Not me! Dey's spirits in dere," he replied.

With Mr. G and the boys gathered around I entered the cave, on my belly, shined the flashlight — and saw something lying on the dark cave floor. It gleamed a soft white — like well-tarnished silver! That's when the flashlight went out. I threw caution to the winds, and started worming my way forward to get a better look.

When I got my head through the narrow part I banged the flashlight against a rock and the beam came on again. I shined it point blank at the pile of silver …and the whitened skull of a goat glared back at me.

As I was wondering whether to laugh or cry, something very soft and feathery, like a piece of moss, dropped on the back of my neck — I reached my hand to brush it off — and it scurried up my forearm — an enormous tarantula with repulsive hairy legs not a foot from my face! My bellow of primordial dread was so loud that Mr. G grabbed me by my ankles and pulled me out "one time!"

Blood ran down my face from scrapes on my forehead. The kids took one look, aghast, and shot off down the path shouting, "SPIRITS! SPIRITS!!"

Mr. G was in a state. "De way you bawl out — mek me skin crawl! Wha' you see in dere?"

"Wrong dream, Mr. G…wrong dream."

5.

DILEMMA AT ORCHILA

A brutal excess of light beat down out of the livid Caribbean sky. Walking on wet sand to keep from burning our feet, we squinted our eyes almost shut against the glare and didn't spot them til we were close. Four big sea turtles lay helpless on their backs, side by side on the beach, just above the line of seaweed that marked high tide. Heat waves trembled in the air above them, even as the sea bounced gently at the shore with cool aquamarine light.

"Look dad...turtles!" exclaimed my older son, Raffy. "But why are they on their backs?" It was the obvious question and one I did not want to answer — a piece of the world's dark freight too heavy for a 9-year-old. I said, "The fishermen must have caught them and left them like that til they're ready to take them to the coast."

He looked at me steadily and asked, "To kill them?"

"Well...I guess so. Unfortunately for turtles, their meat is delicious."

Raffy ran forward and looked into the eyes of the first animal. Its head was retracted into its shell; an infinite sadness gazed back out. He went from one to the other, sighing in pity.

"Their faces are right in the sun. They're not used to it — they're sea turtles, not tortoises! We've got to help them!" He took off his shirt and soaked it in the sea, then ran back and wrung it out on the first animal's face.

Nobody was around. The fishermen had left in their boat at dawn and been gone all day. Their lean-to was the sole sign of human habitation on the long narrow strand that ran for miles, between a vast lagoon to one side and the open sea to the other, and terminated in a distant, barren hill.

The three of us had arrived at this remote outpost — sand, rock, reef and mangroves — at dusk the day before. We were anchored at Isla Orchila, a desert island 80 miles north of the Venezuelan mainland, the last scrap of land before the high seas and our voyage home.

My son had grown up on St. John with a passion for marine mammals. He hoped to see humpbacked whales on our trip but had so far been disappointed. However, turtles were also air breathing marine animals, only slightly below cetaceans on his list of concern, and here were four of them, close enough to pet — and facing death.

"Dad! Ed! Don't you think we should let them go? They're an endangered species. Let's turn them right side up."

"The boy's right," said Ed. Ed knew the Caribbean and its creatures better than most. A self-taught naturalist, he spent his weekends kayaking, snorkeling and camping the outlying cays off St. John.

"These are green turtles — they are on the endangered species list. It's illegal to take them."

"Illegal where?" I asked reluctantly, obliged to be the devil's advocate. "Not here in Venezuela. Every seafood restaurant in Caracas serves turtle steak or soup."

"But dad, it's wrong. They shouldn't allow it. Don't they know that green turtles are endangered?"

"Well, we're not in the States. It's different down here. In South America a lot of people's children are endangered, by poverty. Remember that sea of shacks in the hills above Caracas? Imagine how those people live. The fate of the green turtle is not one of their priorities."

Ed replied, "That's OK for them — but we each have to act on our own beliefs in this world, don't we?"

"Absolutely...but one of my prime beliefs is not interfering with an honest man's livelihood. These guys have families to feed...they get good money for turtle. Maybe this was their lucky day and they're going to buy shoes for their kids with the proceeds. It would be another story if they were sports fishermen or some factory ship — then I wouldn't hesitate."

"So...we do nothing?" said Ed, his face tightening.

"Well, the right thing would be to buy them. You got any money left?" It was a rhetorical question. We had used the last of our money to buy supplies for the trip back. Next stop was home.

"You mean we just have to let them suffer?" cried Raff in disbelief.

"Let's pour some more water on their shells, Raffy. That'll cool them down," suggested Ed, finding a rusty bowl near the fishermen's lean-to. We scooped up seawater and soaked them, feeling a strong empathy with these stoic beasts. Their sad eyes and wrinkled leathery skin seemed ancient and wise, almost human.

We looked around inside the lean-to. It was pretty basic. Crooked poles with bits of peeling bark held up a patchwork tin roof. Three walls of thatch kept out the wind and opened onto the sea. We saw a pile of nets, a coal pot sitting on dead embers, and a kerosene lantern atop a driftwood table. Strings of salted fish and stingray hung drying, and a hammock was slung between two walls. Outside, a barrel held fresh water.

Oil-rich playboys they weren't, nor big time commercial operators — this was a typical camp of the coastal fishing people. My wife and I had met some of them on previous trips — they were warm hearted, family oriented, and generous with the little they had. Though poor, they enjoyed a distinctive way of life on the sea in their rakish boats and in tiny villages nestled into pretty coves along the coast.

We walked back to where our 28-foot sloop rode at anchor. Ed was glum and uncommunicative. I was torn — I had a gloomy hunch they had been caught on the beach while they laid their eggs, and remembered a night spent watching on another island, a mid-Caribbean speck, where turtle after turtle had appeared at the ocean's edge, like black boulders moving out of the dark surf. The memory stayed with me, of their painstaking clamber out of their element, huffing as they heaved their great weight forward up the low beach with their flippers. It remains one of nature's ennobling mysteries how turtles find their way across oceanic drifts of wind and current to the very spot of their birth to lay their eggs. It hurt to imagine them, at the culmination of a thousand-mile migration, to be laid by the heels by waiting fishermen.

As we neared our boat, a flock of flamingoes suddenly flew out of the western glare. They wavered slowly over the tree-tops, their broad wings glowing bright pink in the softening afternoon light, and landed in the shallows of the lagoon.

Shortly thereafter we saw the fishing boat come chugging slowly back to anchor. It looked battered but serviceable, its exhaust smoking, its planking showing at the seams, its cabin top covered with styrofoam floats carrying scraps of flag on sticks to mark their nets and lines. Through binoculars we watched three men scrub down the deck, stow gear, then throw a net in a small dinghy, and row to shore. Soon a plume of smoke arose from the lean-to and we could imagine them eating fish and rice — the same as our own dinner that night — while mending their nets by lamplight.

After supper we sat in the cockpit and looked up at the sky. With no moon, it was a canopy of black velvet, rent in a million tiny places where the back glow of creation shone through. The only manmade light came from the lean-to where the fire still smoldered.

"I wonder if they noticed our footprints around their place," spoke up Ed, who had been quieter than usual. A little later Raffy asked, "Do you think they'll feed the turtles?"

"I doubt it," said Ed. "They eat turtle grass and jelly fish — you can't open a can of dog food for them."

"Then they must be starving!" expostulated my indignant son. "Those fishermen are bad. They deserve to be poor!"

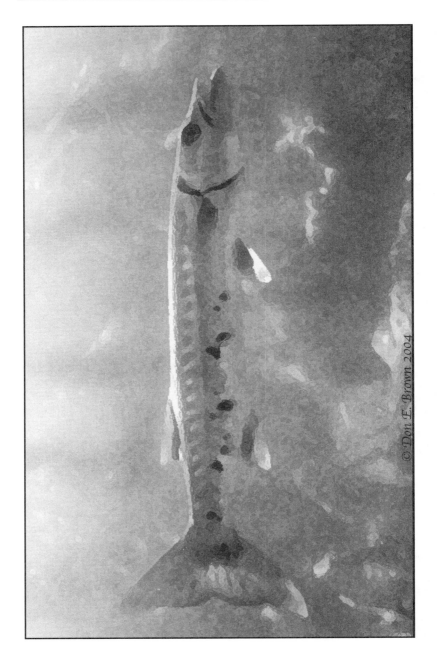

© Don E. Brown 2004

"Raffy, think about it," I objected. "If they killed the turtles now the meat would spoil before they got back to the coast. Turtles can last up to a month on their backs. And I'll bet if you asked the turtles, they'd rather starve and bake in the sun than get their throats cut right now. Maybe the boat taking them to the coast will sink."

"I hope it does! Wouldn't that be cool!" We all imagined for a moment the turtles swimming joyfully off into their element while the fishermen floundered at the surface — on their backs now.

"In the old days when turtles were abundant, sailing ships used to store them on deck so they could have fresh meat a month out at sea. It helped keep away scurvy and probably saved a lot of lives. Turtle fishermen lived on cays like these, and kept their catch alive on the beach to sell to passing ships. It's a time-honored practice."

"Well they should keep them in the shade, at least."

"You're right. But it's funny. When you are planning to kill something, being concerned for its comfort is an awkward thought. You're admitting that it has feelings and emotions. That doesn't help a fisherman."

"Or a soldier," interjected Ed.

There was a silence as we mulled things over.

"My teacher showed us a picture of calves being raised their whole life in little boxes. That's cruel too...and that's in America."

"You like cheeseburgers, don't you?" teased Ed, a vegetarian.

"Well...but it's not...it's not..."

"Don't worry — at least you don't eat puppy dogs, like the Chinese."

"Anybody who would kill a puppy is a murderer!" quavered Raffy, suddenly close to tears.

"And guess what the French eat?" I quickly put in. "Snails and frogs! It's complicated, son... people kill to eat. That's the bottom line. Except Hindus, who don't eat meat? They believe that violence won't stop until we stop killing animals. It does make a certain sense."

"What are we supposed to eat then?"

"Tofu and bean sprouts."

"Yuck!"

Ed laughed and made up his bed on deck. "See you guys in the morning." He sounded cheerful again.

The morning dawned bright and cloudless. Raff and I ate a quick breakfast and went ashore to photograph the flamingoes while Ed stayed on board to get the boat ready for a noon departure.

In the mangrove lagoon the early light brought out the green of the leaves and lent a rich sienna burnish to the tangled roots. Bands of emerald water encircled sandbanks of finely washed gold. We found the flamingoes wading on a sand bar that was barely awash, which bright water skimmed like a mirror, reflecting plump pink bodies and stilt-like legs.

The time whizzed by as we stalked the birds by sea and by land and shot all our film, both of us completely absorbed. Finally, several hours after our noon deadline, we arrived back at the boat, exuberant, eager to stay at least one more day.

"What do you mean, another day?" Ed said, visibly agitated.

"Well, we want to bring some more film and try some different angles. This is the chance of a lifetime. You should come with us."

"Wait a second! I thought we were in such a big hurry to leave. I've got the boat all stowed, took off the sail covers...let's go!"

"What's the rush, Ed? I'm the married man. Raff's the one who's missing school. You don't even have a job. All this trip you've been wanting to linger. Now we get to the greatest place yet and you can't wait one more day?"

"Besides," said Raffy, "I found a jellyfish on the beach. Do you think the turtles would like it?"

"That's just it," said Ed, grimacing with impatience.

"Just it what?" I demanded.

"The turtles!" said Ed.

" You...you turned them over?" cried Raff, a wave of delight cresting in his face. Ed turned to me, defiant, and nodded.

"I swam ashore and went to look at them again...and...I had the power to save them. I was their only chance. If I just walked off, I would feel personally responsible for their deaths. So I turned them right side up. It was worth it to see them chugging down the sand, and then, once they were in the water, streaking towards the deeps. Such beautiful creatures..." he trailed off, and glanced nervously at the horizon again. Suddenly I understood.

"Lord! The fishermen! They'll be getting back soon!"

"Exactly. I thought we'd be long gone by now."

"Well, we're gone now. Get up the anchor...Raffy, turn on the engine!"

We steamed out of there at full throttle, raising sail as we went.

I imagined how the fishermen would curse us — gringos on holiday who despoiled honest workingmen and then snuck off like thieves in the night. They were right, of course. Who were we Americans after all, to tell them what they should do? Our tuna nets had destroyed countless turtles, our resorts had paved over prime beach nesting sites. Now we urged others to do better.

But Ed was right too. He had carried out his convictions and taken the full moral weight of the decision. With him, the turtles had to come first, and let the chips fall where they may. I couldn't muster up a word of reproach. I was glad he'd acted.

It allowed the turtles to live and me to retain a clear conscience. I thought to myself I would return the next year, find the fishing boat and make it up to them, pay them the value of four turtles. I did return several years later and kept an eye out along the coast for them. I even visited Orchila, only to be briefly arrested by the Venezuelan Navy, which had put the island off limits. I never did find the boat again.

God would have to make it up to the fishermen.

Once clear of the island's reefs, we turned off the engine. Our little sloop heeled to a gust and started forging its way home. Raffy had a far away look on his face as he gazed back at Orchila, in rapt communion with the turtles. In his vivid mind's eye, he followed them as they grazed contentedly on a thick bed of turtle grass ten fathoms down, then glided up through translucent indigo to break the surface for a sweet breath of air.

Ed and I watched the fragment of land diminish and disappear.

6.

NAVIGATING DOG

Dog owners are notoriously partisan. A friend of ours had a yellow lab that would spend hours barking at a rock, yet its owner swore by its intellect. Few will admit they have a dumb dog — except owners of Irish setters.

Thus I scoffed when I heard it claimed, by schipperke fanciers who knew nothing about boats, that in medieval times these dogs used to help the barge captains navigate. My professional sailor's ego resented such a frivolous reference to the great art. And anyway, a navigating dog? I liked my dog a lot, thought he was pretty smart, but had no need to assert that he was capable of coastal piloting or dead reckoning.

However, Santos surprised me one dark and nasty night in the far out islands of the Bahamas. Now I'm a believer — not that dogs will ever get proficient with a sextant or even learn to punch buttons on a GPS. But there is no question that dogs have senses that surpass ours, which can be invaluable when traditional navigation techniques fail.

Santos was mightily bummed when we so abruptly left the French Cays, in the central Bahamas.

These two small islets soar to the surface but barely break it — just a rim of beach and a rise of hardy scrub protrude from the sea. Yet they offer a pleasant lee in settled weather and so there we lay, swinging from two hooks set wide apart along the narrow sandy shelf, enjoying the calm days and the radiant water. The shallows showed pale green, the boat floated in three fathoms of blazing turquoise, and fifty yards behind our stern the drop-off plummeted to the ocean floor where the sea reflected a Homeric shade of blue...almost purple.

A southeast wind had led us there from Castle Island and then died away, so we anchored and waited for the wind to return. As far as Santos was concerned, there was no rush — he would happily have spent weeks here. He was by now a connoisseur of beaches and this one was a beauty. People rarely came here, except the passing yacht or fishing smack, so the sand had no footprints save those of lizards and birds, and now and then the tracks of a nesting turtle.

Our last day there unfolded much as the others had. In the morning Santos leapt out of the skiff the instant it slid onto the shore, put his nose to the sand and ran full tilt down the beach, omnipotently flushing sandpipers and red-legged soldier birds into the air.

He played chase-me games with the boys, tearing up the beach with joyous abandon, then went swimming. In the afternoon he accompanied us on a diving trip to the nearby reefs, riding in the front of the skiff — always and without exception in the very front — his rear up in the air and his head low between his paws over the bow, intently watching the bottom speed by in flashes of bright coral and darting fish.

We dove for our supper, gliding down through gin-clear water to ancient coral reefs where thickets of glowing golden elk horn grew atop labyrinthine mounds of dead fragments. Taking a deep breath and diving down 40 feet brought on a rapture which spread the longer one lay on the cool corridor of rippled sand and peered into a shadowy cave at the base of a huge cracked brain coral, increasingly conscious of the weight of the sea above and the play of sunbeams bouncing at the distant surface.

Great groupers wandered up from their deep dark caves beyond the drop-off to prowl the sunlit gardens of coral. A manta ray swam majestically past and looked me in the eye, knowingly. When Raffy discovered a huge lobster tucked into a crevice, a barracuda five feet long and thick as my thigh gnashed a mouth full of needles in agitation at being robbed of a subject. When we heaved it into the skiff Santos attacked it barking and prancing, but the horned monster slithered toward him waving its thorny whips and creaking, and Santos retreated onto the foredeck.

Back at the beach we built a driftwood fire and cooked a feast — lobster and fish, onions, rice and plantains. Santos stuffed himself on lobster in garlic butter, then dug for ghost crabs, his paws furiously showering sand. He thrust his muzzle into the hole, whiffing and sneezing, finally withdrawing with sand everywhere — eyes, nostrils, ears — looking decidedly pleased with himself. The rest of us lay in the lap of the surf, feeling a million particles of sand wash back and forth, softly scouring our skin, as we watched the light fade and throw broad shafts of pink and gold high into the ethereal blue sky. When the sandflies started to bite we packed up and rowed back to the boat.

Since it was the height of hurricane season we religiously checked the evening weather broadcast on the Coast Guard's short wave weather channel. All fall we had been listening to its tropical weather advisories. It had warned us in time to take shelter when tropical storm Isidor hit St. Augustine. Again in the Exumas we'd heard of a suddenly formed tropical depression that made us scramble to find a hurricane hole — which, in the outer Bahamas, are few and far between for a vessel of 6 ½-foot draft. And now, very now, just as digestive lassitude took hold, the radio announced "a strong tropical wave" was headed our way. At its present rate it would arrive in perhaps two or three days.

Now, a tropical wave by itself was no great threat. The danger lay in its potential to develop into something far more powerful — most hurricanes start their lives as tropical waves. Two years ago in Eleuthera just such a "strong wave" had become full-fledged tropical storm Barry overnight and almost wrecked us. We woke up at dawn to 50-knot squalls to find ourselves dragging steadily towards breakers on a lee shore at Governor's Harbor. Our engine was down and if it weren't for the assistance of two Frenchmen who risked their lives in a small Boston Whaler to carry out our last anchor, we'd have been on the beach.

Once bit, twice shy. We had to find better shelter than the glorified sandbars that were the French Cays. Behind us Acklins Island offered nothing suitable to our draft. Much further back Long Island had two small, shoaly, rock-bound harbors — not great, and giving up so much painfully won windward mileage made us cringe, so Mayaguana became our choice. Though it was 40 miles to the east — against the wind — it had Abraham Bay which, if not a hurricane hole, was still our best option to weather a blow.

We had no time to lose. We had to start that night, the sooner the better.

So much for the mellow sailing life, for moon gazing and a sound night's sleep. So much for the sailing fantasy — now we were in for the dark side. Already the clouds seemed less fluffy in the moonlight, the wind less languid.

We prepared for sea, lashing down fuel jugs, stowing items securely above and below. Santos watched us guardedly all the while and when we lifted the dinghy on deck, he lapsed into a doleful resignation. From previous experience he knew it meant a long and potentially rough sail ahead. As he moped, head between his paws, up came the anchors and the sails and within the hour we were underway, rounding the spit of land that sheltered us, driving into the full swell of the open Atlantic.

By midnight the wind had reached Force 6 — well over the misery threshold for a small boat beating to windward in open sea. The clouds had multiplied and lowered, dark squalls appeared on the horizon and bore down, each riding a pillar of rain. Waves mounted, broke, and toppled onto the deck as Breath buried her bow in the oncoming swells. The dismal sluicing of green water on deck sought out every leak in the mast boots and deck prisms and dripped, like a smart bomb, precisely onto my bunk and the chart table. Down below the activated bilge gave off swamp gas while up on deck a blast of exceedingly fresh air flung buffets of spray into unguarded eyes.

© Don E. Brown 2004

Around 3 a.m. the seas got rougher. Suddenly we hit a rogue wave. Like a mean bronco goosed by a cattle prod the boat bucked skyward, then fell off the wave. The motion threw my friend Buddy clean out of his bunk, right over the leeboard, to hit the hardwood floor with a resounding thump. Simultaneously the top of the wave burst against the main hatch, lifting it enough to douse him with about five gallons of sea-water. There was an unprecedented oath of outrage from below — Buddy was the crewmember normally most in control of himself.

Day dawned and waxed and conditions remained rough. The tropical weather update reported the wave steadily approaching but with no further development. The day dragged by slowly, everybody wishing they were somewhere else. Raffy, Buddy and I tried to carry out the normal routine but we were all on the verge of nausea — trying to cook or wash dishes or find some piece of gear stored in the violently thrashing fo'c's'le brought it on, accompanied by pallor, cold sweats, dull headache. Diego and Dorothy, as usual, suffered the worst, and spent the day trying to sleep, huddled together on a mattress on the floor in the main saloon, where the motion was least.

My long-suffering wife, who had regularly gotten car sick as a child, was now as an adult condemned to tossing about on a small boat in rough seas. She complained sometimes but mostly suffered in silence. I went down to commiserate with her and asked her what she was thinking of.

"A house... cottage...I'd be happy in a shack," she quavered, "anything as long as it's on shore... I long for flowers... and solid ground."

Santos wasn't seasick but he wasn't happy. The poor dog alternated between standing hopefully at the companionway hatch, swaying and bracing to the cant and pitch of the boat; and hunkering down in ever more sodden misery in the cockpit, taking what shelter he could, wincing as the bow crashed against another oncoming box car and the inevitable lash of spray found him. He was the picture of misery, eyes woebegone, fur bedraggled. We tried to cheer him up but he'd barely lift his head, and then only to give us a deeply reproachful look. He desperately wanted to go below but because it had been a day since he'd been ashore to relieve himself he could not be trusted. The atmosphere in the cabin was rank enough already.

By now we had to be close to Mayaguana but because it had been too cloudy to take sights (this was before GPS revolutionized the practise of navigation) our position was based solely on dead reckoning, the process of artfully guestimating a vessel's position (which the Spanish call "por fantasia" — wonderfully apt to the English ear.) The chart warned that local currents were quite variable, much affected by wind. How much to allow for drift? I had carefully reasoned estimates, but they could be way off — which in these waters could be disastrous. Mayaguana was low, sparsely lit, fringed by reefs.

We hoped to fetch its lee sometime after dark. By 10 p.m. I was getting perturbed. We should see something, feel something, a slackening of the sea. Could I have misjudged the currents so badly that we might run into the five-mile reef? Or, more likely given my caution, would we sail far short of it and go right by in the night, too distant to see any light or feel any lee?

As my calculations revolved yet again in my head, a remarkable change wrought itself in our dog. He was pricking up his ears, lifting his head, and twitching his exquisitely sensitive nose. For a moment he stood hopefully, then, with a despondent sigh, sank back down in dank misery.

But five minutes later he leapt to his feet and stood with his tender nose ardently thrust into the corrosive wind and spray. His whole body quivered like he was electrified. A whimper of the utmost longing issued from his throat. Something windborne possessed him absolutely. What else could it be but the edge of land? We must have reached it and the island's scents of dogs and salt ponds and pungent shrubs had mesmerized him.

He convinced me, at any rate. Land! We dropped the jib and strapped the other sails in tight and motor sailed hard upwind in short tacks, 15 minutes on each board, following directly up Santos' olfactory bearing. Our little pilot continued to shake eagerly, heedless of the spray, as we neared the source of his revelation. Gradually we felt the seas subside, and after 90 minutes we picked up the Mayaguana light at Betsy Point.

From there on in it was a piece of cake. The approach was deep and clear and we eased in carefully to the roadstead close under the low cliffs where the light stood. When we could see ripples in the sand below we dropped the hook and lay back gratefully. We opened the hatches and let the wind blow through the cabin, dispelling in a trice all the dankness of the trip. We took fresh water showers, changed our sheets and opened a bottle of wine. Then we turned in, once again in a euphoric mood. From our bunks we could see, framed by the hatch, bright stars in the velvet night.

If it weren't for Santos we would have passed the island unwittingly and still be heaving around wet and lost on the high seas. His nose was better than an Radio Direction Finder — just as accurate and much less likely to blow a fuse. It gave us a rudimentary but essential bearing.

This experience provided us an insight into the schipperke's historical place on boats, which reaches back perhaps as far as the Hanseatic League. What worked for us must have worked even more for the medieval skipper, who sailed without electronic aids. The dogs' acutely augmented senses — especially sound and smell — would have been the next best thing to radar. Santos' compulsion to bark at other dogs on boats, seen in this light, might have been a form of echo location — two dogs barking as their boats approached each other on a foggy morning coming to a bend in the river.

As for the tropical wave, seeing that we had paid our dues and shown sufficient respect, it proceeded past us with an impressive display of lightning, and sheets of rain, but did us no harm.

7.

ANIMAL WARS

When we sailed in to Round Bay and dropped the hook in the sheltered cove off our old house, we were finally back at home. It was the end of 1984 — we had been gone almost two years. Breath had performed her maiden voyage without a hitch — she was solid as a rock. And Santos had passed the test with flying colors — he'd done his duty and proved good company. His place aboard Breath was assured.

However, his place on shore was not so assured. There were other animals already there — dogs, donkeys, goats, mongooses, cats — who felt they had rights. If he wanted to claim his birthright as The Dog of The People who lived there, he would have to look lively.

Fortunately, looking lively was his stock in trade.

When Santos got there the road had been newly paved but it was still used more by the donkeys with their fluffy, wide-eyed foals, than by the people. Hours might go by without seeing a car.

Although a newcomer, Santos jumped to the top of the animal hierarchy. As the only dog of the only family in the cove he was prince of beasts. Among the wandering herds of goats, the itinerant donkeys, the mourning doves, the bold thrushies, the stray cats and wild dogs and sly skulking mongooses — he alone had an official position, with duties — and privileges —

to match.

Alone among these kindred he had a guaranteed subsistence, above all else the assurance of as much fresh water as he could drink — no small thing when drought afflicted the island.

And as for his duty, why it was nothing less than to take charge, to guard the premises, to run some animals off the property and see to it that the other animals toed the line while they were passing through. He was to be the policeman. It was a job made in heaven for a schipperke, whose name means "little captain" in Flemish.

Santos had his work cut out for him, though, because many of the animals felt that the old house under the giant tamarind tree was their own domain. Especially the goats and the donkeys considered themselves aggrieved. After all they had already been there, living in the bay and in the house when we first arrived. The history here went back years before Santos' arrival, but he was come to set it right.

Before East End we had been living on Lovango Cay. It had given us four wonderful years but it was time to move on. We needed a more convenient place to build Breath, somewhere with electricity, phone and some sort of access by road.

While working in Coral Bay I heard from a friend about a dilapidated but potentially serviceable dwelling at the end of the road at East End. It had lain abandoned for several years now after its last tenant, an old eccentric hermit, had died. Most relevantly, it was still hooked up for phone service and electricity and had a piece of flat ground beside it, next to the water, where a boat could be built, then easily launched. In fact, boat building had flourished there a century ago.

So one day I borrowed a skiff and bounced out to East End and beached the boat at the head of a deeply scalloped cove, where the sea barely moved against the sand. The quiet cove shimmered a deep blue. The wind rustled the old gnarled tamarind tree softly and one could hear the gentle clear coo of mourning doves. The house lay in the sun, sagging, its roof rusty and partly overgrown by a lime tree whose branches and fruit lay piled in the rotting gutter.

I walked into the yard and let the vibes soak in. The place was perfectly peaceful, the sunshine warm, the grass thick, the air buzzing with the distant drone of bees. I loved it right away. There were no neighbors in sight, none in the whole cove. It was ours if we wanted it.

Then a clomping sound came from within the house, a muffled thump, and out the doorway poked a gray muzzle and long fuzzy ears — a donkey. When I approached for a closer look, out burst a troop of them, hawing and snorting suspiciously, stomping on the ground, sending up little puffs of dark dust from the charcoal-saturated ground.

The house was classic West Indian, 70 years old, two rooms under an artfully framed hip roof whose rafters were routed and whose joints were all mortised and tenoned by hand, During its early years, it had been a rum shop, where people came in with an empty jar to fill from a barrel of transparent volatile spirits that smelled like jet fuel. (So much so that, years ago, when a barrel fell off a barge and washed ashore, the people on a small island in the Grenadines, thinking it was some kind of high proof spirits, broached the barrel — with fatal results. Instead of high proof it was high test.)

But by now it was considered uninhabitable, because the goats and donkeys had been living in the house like it was theirs.

We had to wash and scrub the whole house time and again with bleach and strong soap, then leave it all to air out, then close all the doors and shutters and go inside to sniff. Three times it smelled and three times we scrubbed it harder, with ammonia, carbolic acid and a thick solution of baking soda. Finally even Dorothy's sensitive nostrils were satisfied and we began to paint. The interior had been dark gray with a turgid maroon trim — whatever colors the hermit had been able to score. We painted it white and cream and pink and the effect was extremely pleasing.

The goats, dumb as sticks, accepted their eviction order with resignation but the donkeys were another story — they put up a struggle that amazed us and demonstrated their considerable intelligence. They kept trooping by while we worked on the house, stomping their feet at a distance and harumphing disdainfully and generally keeping an eye on our progress, waiting for the moment to make their move. They must have tapped their collective unconscious for a folk memory of the Musicians of Bremen. How else to explain their inspired tactics the very first night we actually slept in the bedroom?

Feeling very satisfied with the smell of fresh paint faintly lingering, new screens keeping out the bugs, our new home all scrubbed and clean, Dorothy and I drifted off to sleep in the bed I had just built.

Half an hour after our lights went out, four donkeys crept up and silently gathered directly outside our screened bedroom window, their muzzles placed together not five feet from our ears. One moment we were sleeping peacefully, lulled by the sweet sounds of the East End night — a few crickets, the lap of wavelets on the beach — the next moment an earsplitting bray, the most atrocious sound in the animal kingdom exploded our sleep. Delivered point blank in unison worthy of the Tabernacle Choir, this cacophonous blast of jackass breath had the effect of a cattle prod to the crotch.

Our bodies levitated quite clear of the bed, as every nerve and sinew clutched in simultaneous spasm. Then the source of the unmistakable sound registered and the millisecond of sheer terror gave way in rapid succession to relief, outrage, and grudging admiration like a white-water raft bumping over fast rapids.

They continued braying at the top of their lungs. I burst out of the screen door and one of them bolted off, but three of them weren't budging — a grizzled, weather-beaten old male and two of his life-long harem. With their lips wrinkled away from their strong buck teeth, and with their long ears laid flat back against their necks, they stamped at the gravel and brayed so violently they must have confused their fables and meant to blow the house down.

I bellowed back, to no effect. I reached down and picked up a pebble. They ignored me. "The nerve!" I thought, and heaved the stone hard at the male's flank. It bounced, with a little puff of dust. They stopped braying but still stood there, looking at me stubbornly. I grabbed a handful of pebbles and flung them, peppering the animals. They reared back and snorted but obviously the pebbles hadn't made enough impact. I scrabbled around in the dirt for something sizable and hurled it hard at the male's haunch. He flinched a little, regarded me with scorn, but cantered away as I pelted bigger rocks at their backsides.

I came back to bed less than triumphant — they were still braying just out of rock range, my hands were dirty and my breath agitated. But my indignation gave way to Dorothy's amusement.

"My hero!" she cried, holding her arms open for my return and I had to laugh, considering how cleverly the donkeys had timed their attack.

Nor had we won the war. Persistent campaigners, the donkeys visited us nightly for almost a month. The next night I sprang outside and scrabbled in the dirt and the dark for a rock that was sufficiently big to make it felt through those tough hides. I grabbed impulsively at a neat pile of round stones and got a handful of fresh donkey droppings for my pains — I swear I heard a bray of derision. Score two for the donkeys, zero for the people.

After a while the donkeys mating season arrived, and the nights were full of brays from the hills and the hard clatter of hooves on the road as the dominant male chased away any horny young contender by clamping powerful teeth onto the skin of its neck.

After the donkeys returned to normal and foals were rounding the bellies of the mares, they discovered advantages in having us humans around. Our laundry water stood around unguarded in our open air wash room during the long spells of drought and we often discovered in the morning that a five-gallon bucket where clothes had been put to soak overnight was empty, soap and bleach and all.

At the same time, the donkeys continued to regard us as usurpers of their homestead, as did the goats, and they always tried to reclaim the old homestead whenever we were out.

© Don E. Brown 2004

Enter Santos. When we got back to St. John and reoccupied the house we felt that finally we'd outsmarted the barnyard animals by bringing one of their own whom we'd co-opted.

Now we had a guard who would keep watch and keep order while we were gone. And so it seemed. He reliably set up a great hue and cry if a goat, or most particularly a donkey entered the yard; often, as we arrived home, we'd see him snapping at the heels of some hoofed intruder, threatening to maim any beast that tarried. We commended ourselves and our high voltage watchdog for his diligence.

But we hadn't reckoned on animal loyalty or Santos' basically live-and-let-live attitude. After a while it became clear that for all his posturing when we were around, when we were gone his regime was considerably less draconian — to say the least.

One day we all drove to Coral Bay in our Toyota pickup for the annual Earth Day cleanup. Now, normally Santos could recognize us coming from a distance by the sound of our truck — he had a keen ear for vehicles — but this time a friend who needed to move some rocks borrowed our truck and we returned home incognito in his Suzuki.

What did we find when we walked into the house but Santos — asleep at his post! — While a troop of goats trampled promiscuously over our floors and a nanny goat with bulging udders had climbed onto the counter and was eating vegetable scraps bound for the compost pile.

We swatted them with a broom out the doorways and they clattered down the gravel path. Santos, after vociferous barking, slunk away shamefaced and disappeared for the better part of the afternoon. Problem was, he never identified goats as a real threat. His main thing with goats was to chase them. That he loved — it was such a rush when he made them believe, even if just for a moment, that he was dangerous.

It had to be done right, he had to appear suddenly out of nowhere — like the time he jumped from the window of our moving truck, and fell like a clap of thunder on a herd of goats browsing by the roadside. With an easy escape route at hand they panicked and bolted, no goat wanting to be the straggler who got mauled.

For a glorious moment Santos was in hot pursuit of some 20 animals all much bigger than he. They bleated and snorted, their cloven hoofs clattered over the gravel, their bodies broke dry branches as they leapt away in headlong terror. Santos nipped at the heels of the laggards, growling in a mighty fury — absolutely loving it.

Then, after the first instinctive flight, a stinking old ram goat, with a long shaggy beard and massive horns curled back like brazen scimitars, his pendulous testicojones in a long leather sack bumping between his knees, would suddenly stop and turn with horns at the ready and stamp at the ground. Santos might make a quick feint to see if it would bolt. But when it was dug in and breathing fire the diminutive dog came to a swift skidding halt and watched calculatingly, then ambled off with his tongue lolling out the side of his mouth in a self-pleased grin.

But it was his relationship with donkeys that showed us what was really operating between the animals. A donkey could not enter our yard without Santos going berserk, springing bolt upright, and his feet scrabbling in a rotary blur on the wood floor till they caught a seam or a knothole that shot him out the door. He'd charge at them as they came loitering opportunistically onto the premises, looking for water or garbage. We'd watch, horrified, as Santos rushed right in under their sharp hooves, within an ace of instant death from a donkey's piledriver kick. Sick with apprehension we'd implore him to come back, but he totally ignored us. The donkeys would snort and bray and lay their ears back flat in displeasure and stamp the ground and grudgingly hobble off.

Yet the funny thing was, they never actually tried to kick him. They had ample opportunity to knock him insensible, clear into the bay if they chose to — donkeys have an extremely swift, accurate and powerful kick, like a hoofed nail gun, but they never used it on him, obnoxious though he was.

It became clear what was going on when I noticed that, as with the goats, if Santos thought we were gone he paid absolutely no attention to donkeys. They could browse as they wished, even come right into our open-air wash room and drink whatever they could find. Santos would lie snoozing, his head between his paws, and scarcely look up. It became clear that he just attacked the donkeys because he felt it was part of his job description when we were around.

Clearly, the donkeys realized that it was his job. They would grudgingly vacate the premises once we showed our face, quite clearly unimpressed and even contemptuous of the little dog's yapping bravado, but nonetheless respecting his right to a livelihood. It was real animal solidarity.

The donkeys helped shape the East End experience. They had once been useful farm animals, beasts of burden carrying people over rough trails or panniers of supplies and produce up and down the hills from the gardens to the sea, but their role had passed, along with the age of subsistence agriculture. Wandering about on their own recognizance they were unfortunately destructive to the horticulture of the island, being fond of whatever people grew.

They lived almost symbiotically with people, feral, not really wild, knowing that there was a connection between their race and man — and that they were owed. They liked to hang around people's houses, ours especially because it had that big shady tamarind tree in our front yard to shield them from the sun, where they could browse around for fallen fruit and feed off the newest leaves. Just across the road lay the most sheltered nook of water and beach in all of East End, with shady trees at the edge of the sand. They appreciated this beautiful spot as much as we did. It was on their route as they foraged and ambled the length and breadth of the peninsula, whose terrain and best views they knew better than any person.

Early one morning I met them on the high road between Francis Bay and Cinnamon Bay. It was just dawn, a soft mist lay lightly on the road and cloaked the donkeys, rain water reflected in the hollows of the asphalt like mirrors set into the road, and a lovely freshness remained in the air from the pre-dawn squall that had swept by, shaking the trees, showering down droplets, and passing on. The donkeys' coats beaded up and sparkled —

they didn't care about the rain being wet or cold. Rain meant juicy foliage, and clean pools to drink from — they were completely at home with it.

One got the distinct impression that the donkeys were purposefully here at dawn to watch the sunrise. Smart and aware, heedless of discomfort, in closest contact with nature... they reminded me of the Spartans. The animal kingdom in the West Indies forms a continuum that starts with whales and ends with the sand fly. Not sure where to put the donkeys — somewhere near dogs....and people.

Santos was up on the bow of the boat one afternoon as we came home from a day's charter. We ghosted in past Pelican Rock, and then a wind gust heeled the boat over in the flat water, her wake seething like champagne. As she approached our cove the long gust died and the air that wafted from shore — his sphere of influence by any standard bore a scent that Santos sniffed at with growing displeasure. Something was amiss on the land. The dog's coat bristled; he began to make his warning noise, a low suspicious "rrruff....rrruff."

By the time the boat eased up to its mooring, Santos was beside himself. Four donkeys were taking the sun and wading in the water and acting like the place belonged to them right on the little sandy beach in the corner of our bay where the dinghy had to land!

The vehemence of each bark lifted him stiff-legged off the deck, his spiky black mane flared — and as the boat stopped to pick up the mooring buoy he gave us a look of sheer disbelief that we weren't going to steam full ahead and plow a furrow up the beach.

But his own duty was crystal clear. He gave a sharp "I've got this covered" yelp, and flung himself off the bow. He surfaced emitting a strangled gargling bark — he had been barking underwater. His four paws pulled urgently for shore; he left a discernible wake widening behind him in the flat blue water.

The donkeys looked up as he neared shore. The closer he got, emitting erratic growls and yelps, the more alert they became, and a little skittish. Perhaps the sight of the black head and the flashing jaws stirred a vestigial warning neuron in the donkeys' brains, a remnant primeval memory of black caimans in an ancient water hole. The donkeys stamped nervously and — just in case — moved back onto the beach enough to get their hooves out of the water.

Santos' feet finally touched bottom, scrabbled for traction, caught against the gravel and shot him out of the water like a sub-launched cruise missile, With his hair wet and clinging he resembled a bedraggled big-eared rat but his mad charge strongly intimated rabies. Whatever the reason — maybe they were visitors from another part of the island — the donkeys suddenly stampeded for the bush.

An unmistakable gloating note laced Santos' victory cry as he plunged into the undergrowth, hot as a poker on their heels. It looked like TV footage from the Serengeti — a herd of fleeing Abyssinian asses pursued by a Napoleonic peccary about to wrestle down the hindermost and rip its throat out.

Then something happened in the bush where we couldn't see. We heard an outraged braying, a prodigious stamping and quaking of foliage, and suddenly they reappeared in reverse order, Santos first with his ears flat back, streaking for dear life across the beach, with the male donkey hot in pursuit, livid with rage, his ears laid flat back along the bulging chords of his neck, his massive buck teeth clenched in hatred, braying an apoplectic curse.

Our hearts in our mouths, we watched the little daredevil leap into the water and swim to safety, just ahead of the donkey's gnashing teeth. The pursuit reared up short at the water's edge and Santos, knowing he was safe, swam back to defiantly bad-mouth his adversary. The donkey gave it up as a bad job and trotted off with his harem.

Back on the boat we fell to the deck with laughter. As we came ashore he swam out to greet the dinghy. We lifted him in and he shook himself all over our passengers, who kept exclaiming they'd never, ever, in all their life seen such an amazing dog.

8.

THE TIRE IRON

The old house we inhabited sat all by itself on a beautiful cove at the end of a long unpaved road. Beautiful...but when we needed something it was a long way into town.

One morning I discovered that not only did my old VW bug have a flat tire, its tire iron was missing too. I searched all through my shop, and the house, asked the boys and my wife, to no avail. Finally I had to trudge up the hill to see if any of my neighbors happened to have a lug wrench that would fit a VW bug. The one I needed was a piece of steel that had a pry bar on one end and a 90-degree curve with a socket on the other end.

It was late in April and the century plants on the hillsides were in full bloom, their masses of tiny, golden yellow flowers dazzlingly vivid against the bright blue sky. Falling down to the sea, the rugged slopes were covered with close-knit, hardy scrub that soaked up the sunlight. Beyond lay islands, and far beyond, the perfect arc of the horizon. Of the components of this beauty I noticed only the heat and the steepness, as I wiped the sweat off my brow, wishing I had remembered to bring a hat before impetuously setting off.

Naturally, no one had a tire iron that would fit. I was going to have to walk and hitch hike into town to buy one. Then I remembered it was a Sunday — and everything was closed.

My life was on hold till Monday.

© Don E. Brown 2004

My mood deteriorated even further. I was in danger of blaming my wife or the boys — somebody! — when I noticed a boat entering our cove. My good friend Bob Gross drove close to shore and called out:

"Hey Peter, want to go diving?"

"I can't — I've been searching half the morning for my tire iron."

"I didn't say driving."

"Yeah, I know…"

"Well if you haven't found it by now you might as well dive up some lobster instead."

He was right. I got my mask and fins and lobster snare, jumped into the boat and off we went, bouncing over the water, feeling the wind in my face and the sun on my back. My mood started to lift. I let myself go with the flow.

We anchored off the east side of Turner Point, a bold peninsula, totally uninhabited with not even a path on it, that juts almost a mile into the sea. Conditions were perfect, the sea was calm, and visibility was excellent, big brain corals beckoned us from where they lay on the bottom in 20 ft. of water. We put on our masks and fins and slipped into water so clear it was like falling into liquid air. Beauty flooded in through our eyes as we dove down to explore promising coral heads and came back to the surface gasping for air.

The diving felt good — the exercise and the deep breathing, the ethereal blue water, the loveliness of the coral. Relaxed now, absorbed in the sport, I took a deep breath and glided towards a large brain coral that had a cave at its base. Putting my cheek close to the sand I looked into the gloom. A red-spotted rock hind peered back, and a platoon of glassy-eyed sweepers patrolled restlessly back and forth, but no lobster. Yet there was something resting on the sand. It was man-made, heavily overgrown with coral, but clearly something long and thin with a curve at one end. In fact, it roughly resembled… a tire iron.

Intrigued, I brought it back to the boat. With a diving knife I started scraping off the coral. I could see it was steel. Bob emerged and watched it take shape — one end was like a pry bar and the other was curved and had a socket. No question...it was a tire iron.

Amazed, consumed with curiosity, we forgot about lobster, pulled up the anchor and Bob fired the boat full throttle over the water back to East End. By the time we got there I had scraped the steel perfectly clean. Handling my find with certain awe, I took it ashore, called Dorothy and the boys, showed them what I had found...and tried it on one of the VW's lug nuts.

It fit. A snug, perfect fit. Stunned, I changed the tire.

Coincidence...? What were the odds?! Some would call it a miracle! Whatever, it left me humbled and wondering.

More may be going on in this world than meets the eye.

9

NADIA THE CAT

Then there was Nadia the cat — she was Bo's charge, his cat, his mouser. Bo, our neighbor at East End, didn't do that well with animals. His big dog, Studly, fell off the porch or jumped, heedless of the rope around its neck, and when Bo got back late one night he had a hanged dog to dispose of. Of course, Bo didn't do the best even with himself. He was big, fair-haired, genial, a great guy, but he did things like drive off the ridge of Chicago Hill when drunk — and survive.

Anyway he had this remarkable feral cat. She was stocky, scarred, missing part of her tail, a dingy gray with darker stripes. Bo had acquired her from the bush, hence she was never quite tame, her feral instincts never far behind. Nadia was not one to greet strangers by rubbing against their legs and purring. You could see the wariness and the veiled hostility just under the fur. Yet having known a human's love and care she had quickly come to expect it as a right. This made for a bad combination — a bobcat's sensibilities with a house cat's sense of entitlement.

She was a surly, skulking beast in the best of times and when Bo left the island, times were not the best. What happened was Bo got badly disappointed in love. He'd been having an exciting affair with a glossy-haired, voluptuous and open-hearted girl whose husband was mostly away, off sailing, caught up in the fast lane, trying to make his fortune. She didn't like being left alone, and she finally turned her attentions to Bo who was strong and handsome, was always there for her and treated her son as his own. However when the husband reappeared, flush with money, willing to overlook her lapse and eager to take her away, they reconciled and went to the States.

Bo lived in a half-ruined West Indian house located up a steep overgrown path that led halfway up the hill behind our bay. A beautiful flamboyant tree overhung the porch and its red blossoms framed a spectacular view of Coral Bay. In this lovely setting the broken-hearted lover's mind seethed with hurt and he wallowed in drink. Although gentle as a lamb when sober, he was a belligerent drunk, especially capable of anything self-destructive.

This was when he rolled his jeep off the side of one of the steepest roads in Coral Bay, tumbled over and over and came to an uptilted stop. Bo crawled out and up — up slopes of sharp, loose shale and through thickets of catch-'n-keep — ever upwards til he finally reached the road, identified a house whose people he knew, and knocked on Jerry's door, at the hour of 2 a.m. Jerry came to the door, opened it and there stood big Bo, bleeding from a dozen cuts and scrapes, dirt all over his face and clothes.

"Jerry!" Bo said, " I need some more Tequila!" Everyone agreed that he only survived because he was drunk.

After he rolled his jeep he realized he needed a change of scenery and so, abruptly, he left; making, of course, no provision for his cat, figuring, if he gave it any thought at all, that she could fend for herself. Which she should have done, being a practiced thief and a merciless killer, in particular of unwary birds. However, instead of returning to the bush to forage for rats and thrushies, she decided to go on welfare and let the people feed her.

Our house was close and not as well secured as our island neighbors', and there it was that she came, skulking around the perimeter, waiting her chance for something to steal. She started off by breaking into the house and eating the dog's food. We couldn't drive her off — she'd grudgingly remove just beyond the farthest distance we were willing to chase her and lurk malevolently in the bush till the coast was clear, then come surreptiously to the kitchen hoping to find a morsel. We'd drive her off when we saw her interloping but she didn't scare off easily. She felt she had a right to be fed and would only grudgingly and slowly give way. She showed no fear.

Now, I should explain that we already had a cat and a dog and a parrot, and had to fend off goats and donkeys and mongooses — and had to deal with finding stray animals, often puppies or kittens that had been driven by their owners to the end of the road and dumped out of the car — a traditional way of disposing of them by people too tender-hearted to drown them and too lazy and cheap to take them to the animal rescue center in St. Thomas — admittedly a hassle in the days before the car ferry. At any rate we had no need or desire for stray animals — we dealt with them all the time. If we welcomed them with open arms we'd have an indefinite number of pets because people were always coming down to the islands in the winter, and then would feel the need for companionship and acquire a dog or cat which they would lavish affection on, then leave. Nadia was a particular peeve because she was ugly and surly and often hungry.

One afternoon we went for a quick dip just in front of the cottage without putting away a large cream pie which Dorothy had just drawn from the oven and laid out on the counter to cool. We were intending to have a large piece of it with our afternoon tea. So, after a brisk swim we strolled back to our dwelling, pleasantly hungry, anticipating a still-warm-from-the-oven pie. What did we see when we entered the kitchen but Nadia, up on the counter, both front paws planted firmly in the pie, her face buried up to her eyeballs — in my pie!

I gave a bellow of outrage and she scarcely looked up, whiskers bowed with cream — there was no guilty start, no panicked bolting out a window — just a calculating glance my way to assess the distance between us, never missing a beat as she inhaled that pie. I reached for the nearest missile — an old shoe

— and heaved that at her. She sidestepped adroitly and jammed her snout back in deep.

I lost it. There was a machete by the door. In a fury I sent it whizzing her way. It passed over her head and stuck quivering in the wall. That she paid attention to — she leapt out the window, bursting straight through the old but heretofore serviceable screen, and disappeared into the bush.

Not for long though. Early one evening, we had gathered around with a few friends in what passed for the backyard of the house, under the stately old boxwood tree where we had a fire going. Over it we had set a piece of iron grating supported by two cinder blocks. On this grill roasted pieces of chicken, and a fat grouper that Raffy had caught spear-diving that morning. The meat sent out a delicious aroma that had us enjoying supper immensely, even before we'd tasted it. Conversation and cold beer flowed as we waited. It was a mellow moment.

Suddenly Nadia appeared, slinking unseen until she leapt into the crotch of the boxwood, from which she surveyed the grill hungrily. Then, with malice aforethought and brazen premeditation she jumped up on the edge of the hot grill and started tearing at the fish.

This piece of in-your-face effrontery stunned us for a moment.

"That's my fish, you miserable beast!" Raff thundered, raising his fist. She flinched, hunkered down to receive a blow but kept eating. Raff was flummoxed — the fist was mostly a threat, but he finally cuffed her briskly off the grill and chased her into the dark.

No sooner had he sat back down and the conversation resumed its normal tempo than she was back, glaring defiance, once again jumping onto the hot grill, tearing at the same piece of fish. Brian, who was Bo's friend and knew Nadia the best, jumped up this time and grabbed her by the scruff of her neck and carried her out proclaiming. "Don't worry, this time she won't be back, guaranteed."

He returned smug. "Rest easy — Nadia won't trouble us again."

"What did you do? You didn't hurt her, did you?"

"Nah, she's indestructible...she might have a headache though — I threw her out as hard as I could over the water and I heard a thump — she must have landed in the skiff, so she's stuck out there fifty feet from shore. I'll rescue her in the morning before she makes a mess of the boat."

That done we settled down to supper, each of us with a filled plate, sitting around the fire, with a second round roasting and dripping fat that flared up satisfyingly with a crackle and hiss. Raffy got up and assiduously turned the meat, especially his fish, saying, "I don't want it to burn but it has to be cooked well. I can't stand half-cooked fish. Another couple of minutes should be perfect!"

He resumed his seat and just as he did there was a rustling in the dry leaves and — lo and behold — Nadia, dripping wet, was back. She gave us a glare that said, "I know my rights!" and leapt back onto the grill and tore ravenously into the same piece of fish. We all were astonished. What a cat! What determination — standing there on the hot grill, still dripping from her swim.

"What are we going to do? Do we have to kill her, for God's sake?"

"To hell with it," said Raff. "Let her have the fish." He threatened the cat with a barbecue fork till she jumped back, then he flipped the mangled grouper towards her. Nadia pounced on it and dragged it off into the night.

We talked it over and decided that until Bo came back we might as well give up and feed her. Dry cat food was cheap, and that way perhaps she wouldn't steal or hunt birds. Dorothy put a bowl out for her every night at a decent remove from the house, and sometimes even added a little gravy or leftovers, and occasionally thought unkindly about thoughtless bachelors, and wondered how long Bo would be gone.

A couple of weeks went by and then one afternoon who should show up but Nadia — with four little kittens in tow. She had brought them to show Dorothy it seemed because she waited til Dorothy came out with her bowl of food before parading out from the shrubbery with her offspring behind her. But when Dorothy went to pick one up it gave a hiss and arched its back — it was wild. Nadia was going back to the bush and training her offspring.

"Suddenly it all made sense," said my wife over the supper table. "The poor thing was desperate. She must have had them right after Bo left and there she was, no food, with those rapidly growing kittens sucking her dry. That's why she was so ravenous. She was forced to forage, and the drought made that doubly difficult."

"She needed that cream pie for her babies!" All was forgiven in Dorothy's mind.

Some time later who should appear but Bo, who had stopped drinking and acquired a lovely girl friend. When they left they took Nadia along with them. Bo settled down, got a great job in the city, married his girl and had a wonderful family . . . and Nadia lived happily ever after.

10.

SANTOS AND THE ELEPHANT

Santos lived well, for just a dog. "Just a dog"... It's funny how the expression, "a dog's life", is synonymous with misery and to "work like a dog" means long hard hours, chained to your work.

Historically, of course, that has been a dog's lot — dependent on man and often abused. Even today, in the impoverished third world the average dog's life is tough: reach out your hand to one and it shies away, more accustomed to being struck than stroked. Worse yet, in the Far East it's as liable to be eaten as to be fed. Elsewhere it is tolerated, remanded to the barest of margins, where it skulks around abjectly anticipating a kick.

However times change and language changes accordingly. In our affluent, pet-prone country "a dog's life" is coming to mean "made in the shade."

Take Santos — how wide a gap yawned between his experience and that of a pariah dog in the slums of Calcutta! His life was far more threatened by excess than by deprivation. Not only was he a first world dog, he inhabited one of the cushiest sinecures of the canine gamut, that of a charter boat dog, a star, playing to boatload after boatload of bemused guests.

Every day, someone aboard, generally female, found him irresistible, cuddled him and fed him morsels from their plate. Santos made it his business at the start of each day to find that individual. For his drink he frequently had iced water cupped in someone's palms from the ice chest; and as for his meals...suffice it to say he supped from the table of the gods — his gods at any rate — that is to say, he got our leftovers.

At the end of a day's charter, I often shook my head and thought — there's a dog that has it made.

Yet never did Santos have it so good as in the five blissful weeks he spent cosseted in the company of two prepubescent girls. Kim and Lindsay devoted themselves to him one summer while we sailed down the island chain from St. Maarten to Venezuela. They spoiled him so extravagantly we feared we'd never get a sensible animal back when they left.

But just when he'd been most pampered and indulged, the little dog faced the challenge of a lifetime on a beach in St. Lucia, and met it with a spirit as keen and tempered as a Toledo blade. Like Hamlet's friend, Horatio, Santos was not fortune's fool; he stayed true to himself, come fair weather or foul.

Breath was tied close to the St. John shore, to attract the interest of tourists driving by. Often they would slow down to look, but one morning I heard an exclamation and the screech of brakes, then the sound of a jeep backing up. Out jumped a tall, athletic man with prematurely white hair, followed by a very shapely brunette and two little girls. He admired the boat, asked me a few questions, and promptly chartered it for a weekend trip to Peter Island. Dispatch in decision-making was typical of U. T. Thompson III.

We enjoyed an idyllic sail that weekend, the kind that persuades people to buy boats. The weather was exceptionally clear, the air pure and luminous, so that we could even see the ravines on the peak of Virgin Gorda. The tips of the distant islands, warped by refraction, seemed to lift off the horizon.

Breath sailed up the Sir Francis Drake Channel, past long rocky ridges where the hardy scrub bush soaked up sunlight like a solar sponge and glowed it back in wavelengths just beyond the frequency of human sight. Gusts of wind fell off the hills, filled Breath's sails and made her rigging hum. Boats are like musical instruments made for the wind and sea to play upon — wind and stringed instruments at once, whose hollow hulls are sound boxes to the ocean.

We reached Deadman's Bay by midafternoon. The sun at our back set the pool of blue water alight, reflected off the flawless sand, glistened on a thousand rustling fronds in the grove of coconuts ashore. We stood into the bay til, a hundred yards off the beach in two fathoms of turquoise we turned Breath's bow into the wind, dropped the sails and glided to a standstill. Only the rattle of the anchor chain broke the rapt silence.

Santos hit the beach sprinting, the kids pelted after him and he led them a merry chase along the hard wet sand skimmed by wavelets, up into the soft dry sand that gave underfoot, then tumultuously into the perfect water. Later Diego took the girls out in the skiff, he proudly at the throttle, the girls demure on the center thwart, Santos poised as always on the prow. They came back glowing.

We had supper in the cockpit as the sun sank beneath the western rim and sent up broad spokes of gold and lavender high into the sky. No swell, no bugs, and the stars shone a magnificent testament to God's good taste. It was prime. The family was sold on sailing, on Breath, on Diego...and they loved the dog.

Tom was a native Californian attorney who'd made lots of money with the California real estate boom in the early '80's. His family lived in the lap of luxury, which he was proud to provide, but he also feared that he was spoiling his women, that his girls would grow up soft, habituated to the ease of affluence. He admired the way we lived in an old West Indian cottage, short on amenities but long on beauty. By the end of the sail Tom had proposed an extended summer cruise down the Lesser Antilles, from St. Maarten to Venezuela.

"A long cruise on Breath is just the thing to toughen up my girls," he told me.

"Is that an insult?"

He laughed. "It's a tribute to your lifestyle...your values. There's just one stipulation,"

"What is it?"

"You have to bring Diego and Santos as crew."

Santos grew glum when he saw the dinghy raised on deck and lashed down while a brisk wind strained the boat at its anchor even in the flat water of Virgin Gorda Sound. We had that worst of seagoing strictures — a deadline in rough weather. We'd been waiting day after day for the weather to improve but the wind only wore itself into a deeper groove and raised a bigger sea. Now we had just two days to get across the Anegada Passage to St. Maarten to meet the Thompsons.

The Anegada Passage can be brutal. Sure enough, as soon as we left the protection of land a steep swell broke against the hull and doused Santos where he lay huddled in the cockpit. He glared at me — he knew who to blame.

Twenty-four hours later, Santos' misery finally lifted at the sight of Terre Basse Point shining in the early sun after a dark train of dawn squalls blew down the Anguilla Channel. In the calm that followed he smelled land. By midafternoon we anchored off Philipsburg where the Thompson family was comfortably ensconced in the best hotel on the beach.

Here Santos' ordeal ended and he came into his reward. Kim and Lindsay, 11 and 9, adored furry animals and brimmed over with unfocused love. Santos happily became the focus, a lightning rod for love, took the full charge and wanted more. Basking in their arms, occasionally heaving a shudder of deep satisfaction, his pink tongue tip protruding from his muzzle, he was the very avatar of teddy bears.

Then they walked him along Phillipsburg's cosmopolitan streets, past Indian shops crammed with duty free electronics, past Chinese restaurants and Indonesian bungalows, American taverns and glass-fronted Dutch hotels whose opening doors let out welcome swirls of cold air, where Santos would call an abrupt halt and sit down on the cool flagstone in the middle of the sidewalk. From there they proceeded to the ice cream shop where the children ordered sundaes and Santos under the table received mouthfuls straight from the spoon, as he remembered the previous day's misery, now past, and reflected on life's ups and downs.

Next stop was St. Barths. We came seething past the

Rockefeller's beach at Colombier, past green hillsides dotted with prosperous red roofs, past the fishing village of Corrosol and dropped anchor at the mouth of the harbor of Gustavia.

Here every morning just after first light, Diego rowed through the anchored fleet and made for the bakery accompanied by Santos who strained at the leash, pulling uphill, till he choked. Diego and the dog would share the first warm croissant and then return in triumph with fresh bread and pastries for breakfast. We consumed them on deck, while the air was still cool and the baguettes still warm, with butter and honey, soft cheeses, pate and good strong black coffee.

In just three days here Santos became a persistent beggar for Camembert cheese. The girls would hold out a cracker loaded with Camembert or pate foix and say, "Santos, sit!" His butt would hit the deck before the word was out the mouth. "Lie down!" and he'd flop onto his belly instantly, never taking his eyes off the prize. At "roll over" he would wriggle on to his back. Soon at the command to sit he would sit, lie down and roll over all in one fluid movement.

I had my reservations about all this luxury — he was definitely getting spoiled — but I figured, what the hell, let him live large when he's got the opportunity.

Then it was off to tour the island by car, Santos standing on a willing lap with his head thrust eagerly out the window. For lunch he had his own hot dog and French fries at a chic beach club; and supper found him behaving exceptionally well under the table of a fine French restaurant on the waterfront as the girls slipped him forkfuls of filet sautéed in an elegant sauce. Diego and I weren't parting with a bite.

A great breeze swept us 40 miles to the next islands. We passed between Statia's perfect volcanic cone, to starboard and the smooth rise of St. Kitts' cane fields to port. The uplands ascended like smooth green velvet until Mt. Misery broke through with a rugged violence suiting its name to tower in the perpetual cloud cap. We passed close below Brimstone Hill bristling with battlements and fortifications, then into the dead lee below the 4,000-foot height of St. Kitts, where only occasional eddies of wind reached around the mountains. The lights on shore winked on by the time we reached the Narrows between St. Kitts and Nevis, where we got back the wind by fits and starts. Finally a stiff breeze found us and laid our rail over and released our wake to glow behind us as the dark silhouette of Nevis blocked out stars ever higher and wider in the SE.

We landed the next morning, near a great weathered log that lay half buried in the long expanse of amber sand. There wasn't a soul around. Nevis hadn't been discovered yet — there were no fancy hotels, no chic vacation villas, just the endless beach backed by miles of coconut grove. Behind and above lay the mountain, the powerful backdrop dominating every vista of Nevis.

Wherever Kim and Lindsay went they brought Santos. He never had so many walks in his life. They cradled and kissed him like a baby. They brushed him at least three times a day. When they went swimming they paddled him around on the surfboard. They loved to dress him up, with a bright bandanna around his neck, a beret on his head and dark glasses atop his muzzle. They even did his nails — shiny red polish with glitter on his jet-black claws and dubbed him "Santi-Wanti...!"

That bothered Diego... and me too. What's in a name? More than we had realized, apparently. It blunted what we most liked in the dog — his passion, his fearlessness. We both thought he looked ridiculous, wandering around like an effeminate beatnik, the shades hanging at a deranged angle.

It reminded me of a merengue singer who had put out a brilliantly original first album — a huge hit throughout the Spanish speaking Caribbean. The cover pictured an earnest young man, dressed in a plain dark jacket and tie, looking self-conscious, expectant, and vital.

When his eagerly awaited next album came out it was a dud, totally derivative. Tellingly its cover showed "the Star" lounging in a satin velvet jump suit, with mirror shades, gold chain, flashy rings, etc. A pathetic example of talent kneecapped by fame.

Santos in his flashy get ups looked like that singer — lolling around all day, being caressed, stroked and fawned over!

Perhaps Diego was feeling overshadowed by the sophisticated strong-willed girls and some part of me was a bit insecure next to the highly successful Tom. Now it seemed like our prized dog, our symbol was losing his edge — defecting to the tapestried tents of the Sybarites and leaving us plain-spun Spartans behind.

We should have known better.

Visible from far out at sea, Petit Piton is St. Lucia's most famous landmark, a massive rock spire that dominates the coast and whose peak floats with the clouds 2,000 feet above the sea. When we got to St. Lucia we anchored in Jalousie Bay, directly beneath the cliffs of the Piton.

The anchorage was very deep, the bottom an underwater mountainside. We anchored and tied stern to the shore. Below our keel the bottom tumbled down a steep slope studded with rocks, golden coral heads and lavender sponges all clearly visible as through blue glass.

The cove was stunning. The flight of sheer rock stopped the breath, it soared up like the fang of a saber-toothed tiger, crowned with glowing foliage and backlit by clouds of silver fleece. Everything at its base served to set it off — sea of blue crystal, beach of fine black sand, groves of palms shining on the slopes about. Close to shore a shapely skiff turned in the zephyrs; on its stern was stenciled "One Love." Next to it tiny minnows leapt out of the sea, their wet bodies flashing an arc of quicksilver.

Even before we anchored, something out of the ordinary was compelling Santos in to shore. He danced with agitation at the bow, scrabbling halfway out the bowsprit as we motored slowly towards shore with the anchor lowered. When it caught and the stern swung around to face the beach he raced back and scrambled out onto the rudder head where he balanced precariously on three feet and beckoned to shore with the remaining forepaw. He trembled and yelped in the prow of the skiff and even before the stem grated on the shore Santos had jumped into the surf, ran up the sand, put his nose to the ground, and started following a trail through the lush grass.

© Don E. Brown 2004

Going from tree to tree and sniffing assiduously, very intent, of a sudden he heard the cackle of poultry. He broke off his research, dashed down the surf line, and then veered up across the sand and into the grass to home in like a low-flying predator drone on a flock of chickens. Hens and chicks exploded away from him just like minnows from a marauding mackerel.

He stood there, Santos the Terrible, panting triumphantly, his pink tongue hanging out in good-natured exuberance.

He resumed his quest disappearing into the tall grass where presently we heard excited barking and indignant squeals. The grass shook as something big passed rapidly through and then out burst a 250-pound sow, running for its life, with Santos exultant at her heels. We marveled at the disparity. Seeing us laughing, she caught herself, came up fiercely all ahalt and, with a flare of fury in her piggish eyes, turned upon the detestable little rodent that had shamed her. Now it was reversed, the sow charging with grim intent, fast in the short run, impressive mass and momentum — and gaining steadily. She would make mincemeat of him with her sharp hooves.

Santos ran flat out, ears back, glancing over his shoulder to gauge her approach. The girls screamed in alarm, and even I had a sinking feeling but there was nothing anybody could do. Our hearts in our mouths, we watched as the raging sow bore down on him, saw Santos look back a last time — laughing! — and adroitly dodge aside while the pig went thundering past like a runaway train, helpless to alter her course. It was bull versus toreador — Santos the elegant, deft, agile tormentor.

Relief for the sow came in the most unexpected form. To the amazement of all, out from the undergrowth and into the clearing stepped — an elephant! A real, live, full-grown Indian elephant. Santos stopped dead in his tracks, dumbstruck with awe. The defining moment of his life had just stepped out of the bush! An incredible — a miraculous! — opportunity had just been handed him. He had to act — all his life had been leading up to this. There was only one possible response. ATTACK!

Barking his ear piercing war cry, he hurled himself, flat out, straight at the mastodon. Santos vs. the king of the jungle!

The elephant reacted like Santos was a rabid rat. It reared back, flared its huge ears, and trumpeted a scream of alarm. Santos snapped at an ankle big as a tree trunk and then at another. The elephant recoiled with revulsion, as if a cockroach had crawled up its trunk. It brought its feet down in a stamp that shook the earth but the lightning-like little dog had already dodged out from under, and then deftly sidestepped the resounding thwack! of the elephant's trunk raising dust right where he had been a split second previously.

Dashing just out of range Santos wheeled and braved his adversary. The dog was more pumped up than ever we'd seen him, barking hysterically and utterly deaf to me. Time after time Santos rushed in underfoot, weaving and darting, counting coup, as the ponderous creature tried to stomp or smack him.

Santos' frenzied barking and the elephant's piercing trumpet calls brought everyone running. Laborers, millionaires, mariners, hair braiders all stood in an arc around the combatants. The absurdity of this David and Goliath show — the manic daring of the dog and the ludicrous agitation of the elephant — had people helpless with laughter, holding their sides, tears streaming from their eyes.

It was Santos' finest hour. One on one, head to head against the largest animal on earth, the elephant — and the elephant freaked!

Santos was tireless, but the elephant became increasingly upset. Its keeper, between sobs of merriment, finally decided to stop the show before the elephant ran amok. We managed to collar Santos on one of his dashes, no easy feat — he gave me a wide berth but a stranger from the next yacht nabbed him. I took him back out to Breath, keeping an adamant grip on his collar till I dropped him aboard. As soon as I started back he jumped the rail and left a wake in the placid water, his eyes shifting from me to the shore. I finally had to tie him in the cockpit.

The elephant was a mild and pleasant beast under normal circumstances. Its keeper showed off its tricks. With a little coaxing it would put its foot on top of a coconut and with an easy shifting of its weight crack it open to get at its milk and meat. I shuddered to think of what could have happened had Santos miscalculated. Although sometimes I wonder...because the very next morning the dog and the elephant met up again and acted like old chums, walking at the shore together, Santos only inches away from the mastodon's huge foot.

A multi-millionaire English brewery owner had imported it from India to be an elaborate prop for a New Year's party on Mustique. Mustique is the exclusive island in the Grenadines where the international jet set has their magnificent villas. This party had the British Raj as its theme, giving all the guests — rock stars, models, wastrel nobility, assorted super rich and their sycophants — a chance to wear their biggest diamonds and dress sleazily, as belly dancers, and concubines.

After the party the elephant was put to pasture at the coconut plantation beneath the Petit Piton that the beer magnate also owned. There it was looked after by the same young man who'd been dressed as its keeper in the party — he had the pictures to prove it. For a number of years it amazed yachtsmen who put in to the anchorage and saw, after a couple of drinks, an elephant wandering the shore. Was this Africa or the Antilles? Or the rum?

Later I heard that it had died prematurely and I wasn't surprised. They are sociable beasts and being uprooted from home and kindred and cast into lonely exile in a strange land, a one-time party prop and an ostentatious curiosity thereafter, must have done for it.

Before we left I went up to visit it in its stall, to give it some peanuts, but it never noticed me...it was lost in a private misery, pacing one step forward and one step back in an endless nervous rhythm.

It was an eerie and depressing thing to see and I left the peanuts on the floor.

11.

SOMBRERO

We left Gorda Sound in sunshine and smooth seas, bound for St. Maarten, but by nightfall an easterly swell moved in, the moon and stars were stifled in wet squalls, and it blew 25 knots and worse dead against us. Our small sloop staggered on to windward under a double-reefed main and small jib and, sometime after midnight, fell off a particularly bad sea with an audible crack. The bilges began to need frequent pumping.

We were miserable and getting worried. Unsure of our position or progress, we contemplated running back for the shelter of Virgin Gorda. Then, from the crest of a lurching wave, the helmsman caught a glimmer of light and caught it again — the Sombrero beacon. In an instant our perspective brightened. We knew where we were; St. Maarten was closer than we thought. Until dawn, Sombrero kept flashing us its double wink of courage, and by the next evening we were seated at the old Hong Kong Restaurant in Phillipsburg, cheerfully recounting our ordeal.

But Sombrero has not always been such a friend. For centuries it lay across the Anegada Passage like a stone knife with a chipped edge, in wait for ship's blood. One stormy night in the 1870's, a British liner trying to steer well clear of it hit Anegada's Horseshoe Reef instead, and sank. Hundreds of people drowned or were battered to death against the sharp coral.

England's Trinity Lighthouse Service then erected the first beacon on the deadly rock and has kept it burning steadily for well over a century — one of the cardinal marks of the Caribbean.

"Sombrero? What do you want to go there for? It's just a dung-covered rock with no anchorage and no inhabitants," people told us; but the more they demurred, the better it sounded. No people? Better for the wildlife. No anchorage? No other boats. And what's a boat for, anyway, but to take you away from everything and then bring you back again?

The five of us who went on this return trip to Sombrero aboard Breath, my 42-foot gaff ketch, shared the same idea of a good time: a long week-end on the sea. We even went with a mission. Rob, an ornithologist, suspected that we would find black terns on Sombrero, and if we did, it would be a first for the northeast Caribbean. Buddy was from St. Thomas, Maduro from Tortola, and John and I were longtime residents of St. John. John and Maduro hit it off immediately, like spark and tinder, setting off one blaze of laughter after another as we weighed anchor at noon one Friday and tacked up the Sir Francis Drake Channel.

We passed green islands and golden beaches, and by dark entered the Anegada Passage, well clear of the grasping claws of the Horseshoe Reef. Night fell very clear. The brilliant glow of the universe shone through every star in the velvet sky.

Perfect sailing doesn't usually last for long, and midnight brought a wind shift that forced us to motor sail to fetch our course. Soon the boat slammed and bucked over the rising seas. We shut the hatches to keep out the spray, and the air below grew stuffy and nauseating.

Maduro appeared in the companionway looking pale— unusual in one of African descent — and gulped for air like a beached fish. He curled himself around the mizzenmast, oblivious to the blasts of spray and showers of cold rain, and appeared dead. Others were similarly afflicted, and the rest of the night turned out to be no fun. We spotted Sombrero's light before dawn, followed the bearing, and by the time the sun had climbed high enough to strike bright color into the water, we arrived, eager for the lee.

Sombrero, the northernmost island of the Leewards and the Lesser Antilles, is a stone sliver three quarters of a mile long, a few hundred yards wide, and some 40 feet high. The sea pounds its windward coast, sending up brilliant plumes of spray. Seeing the heavy swells, I wondered if we'd be able to find an anchorage. I climbed the ratlines for a look from aloft. Set broadside against wind and sea, the island parted the waves neatly, leaving a sort of vacuum directly below the cliffs, where flat water sparkled in the sun. We nosed cautiously into it and anchored bow and stern close under and parallel to the cliffs.

We launched the skiff and began looking for a way up. As far as we could see, the island was unbroken cliff, but bolted into the rock, about halfway along the island's length was a shiny aluminum ladder, reaching from just above the sea to the top of the cliff. There a quiet, unblinking face watched us. The island was inhabited after all, and Samuel Richardson, one of Sombrero's resident light keepers, gave us a sincere greeting once we had clambered to the top.

He showed us around his domain. The island's surface resembled a moonscape — desolate and harsh, dominated by craters and fractured rubble. A phosphate-mining company had blasted and drilled for fertilizer back in the late nineteenth century, and old buildings, roofless and beaten to their knees by the elements since then, still showed where men had lived and worked.

In contrast, the lighthouse operation imposed a naval order. Smooth concrete walkways connected all the strategic points — the shop and generator shed; the helicopter pad; the boathouse, with its brightly painted Anguillan longboat running on rails to the sturdy cliffside derrick that lowered and raised it when the sea was calm enough. The snug living quarters felt like cabins on a stone ship, every window opening out to an unbroken horizon. I wondered what it would be like to be there in a hurricane.

We met the rest of the crew. All were Anguillans and spent their two weeks vacation every two months back home on that island, the nearest inhabited land. All had worked on Sombrero 10 years or more, their captain for over 20. A quiet reserve marked them — the work must attract such men or mold them. The cook produced cups of tea for us, and we sat around, awkwardly at first, while the men gazed at us shyly.

Then Maduro started to perk up.

"Well boys," he said reverently, "I got to respec' you for true." He shook his head, impressed. The men looked blank.

"I mean, I try to follow the Good Book, too...you know...but I can't call myself a man of God. Not like you all." The men looked at each other wonderingly. After a pause the comic continued.

"I 'spec you is a priest, right?" he asked the youngest man.

"Who me? No suh!" he blurted.

"Then you studyin' to be a priest?"

"Not me." He shook his head emphatically.

"Let me see...you ain't no priest...and you ain't studying to be no priest...?" Maduro rocked back in mock amazement. "Then how a strong man like you could live on this rock with no woman in thirty miles?" It took the guys a moment to comprehend that this was a joke; then they started to laugh, slapping their thighs and wiping away tears of joy.

We left Maduro working a rapt audience and could hear intermittent howls of laughter borne to us by the wind. The rest of us picked our way over the tortured slag, deeper into the realm of the birds. They loved the craters, many of which were 20 feet deep and larger in diameter. Here the various terns nested on bare rock and sat through rain and shine. The crater walls blocked the wind, and the rock absorbed heat all day to emit it back at night.

If we started down into one of the craters, its residents stared at us balefully and started flapping awkwardly up the sheer sides until they cleared the rim. Then they soared off on the breeze, in their element, sure and graceful. The air overhead was full of them — brown noddies in rich chocolate plumage, roseate and royal terns with their jet-black caps, and bridled terns looking like charcoal on snow. Twice Rob pointed out black terns, but they were never close enough for us to be positive they weren't the similar sooty terns.

© Don E. Brown 2004

To the east there was more cover and fewer craters, and here the larger boobies had staked out their turf. We saw families in every stage — mothers sitting on eggs, chicks, fledglings boldly exploring the rocks and shrubs. At first we saw only the common brown booby. Then Rob nearly dropped an egg he was measuring with calipers as he exclaimed: "Look! Masked boobies. They're not supposed to be here!"

If so, nobody had told them, for quite a few pairs with chicks dotted the uneven ground. We walked right up to them. These birds were all white with the exception of a broad black band along the trailing edge of their wings. A cowl of fine feather work close above their vivid yellow eyes gave them the look of mad monks. I moved with camera to within three feet of a chick, a study in fluffy white innocence. Its parents took a dim view of my intrusion and threatened me with great dignity, hissing and pecking their long sharp beaks at the air.

We walked back along the seaside cliffs watching the sun descend. Back at the lighthouse, I asked what would happen if a hurricane struck. From the men's expressions I could tell this was a significant question. Automatically they turned to Niles, who had been on the rock when Hurricane Donna hit the Leeward Islands in 1960 without warning, packing winds of over 150 knots. It marked the passing of an era; the entire trading schooner fleet of Anguilla and St. Barth's was wiped out, and tourism began to change the face of the islands soon after.

Niles was 17, working with a crew to erect a new steel light tower. The foreman then, an old Anguillan seaman, didn't need a weather satellite to interpret the leaden calm and long swell, followed by heavy black clouds on the horizon. Two of the men holed up in the old masonry tower while the rest of the crew barricaded themselves in the main living quarters.

The wind rose, the seas broke on the top of the rock, and water washed completely over the island. With three feet of seawater standing on the floor of the living quarters, the men climbed into the window apertures of the 4-foot thick stone walls. Then they heard a phenomenal sound approaching, a roar that rose over them and engulfed them, as, with a paroxysm of total power, a monstrous sea broke into the building's roof and demolished it. Only their places in the window apertures saved them from falling debris. The two men in the tower gave themselves up for dead when a similarly enormous comber obliterated their roof and plucked them out into the chaotic night.

In an incredible coincidence, one of the men was washed high into the air, and then dropped through the open roof of the main building and left, half-drowned and injured, in a pool on the floor. His mates dragged him to safety. The other fellow was swept past the building by one wave, and then sucked back by the ebb. He managed to climb through a broken shutter into the pantry and tumbled out when the storm abated and the cook opened the door.

The newly erected steel tower was blown down. Later the crew put the tower back up and built a massive supporting base with four immense pillars of reinforced concrete. They meet in a pillbox with window slits that sit 75 feet above sea level — the refuge of last resort for Sombrero's light keepers.

Next morning, when day had properly asserted itself, John and I went diving — not scuba, but with fins and masks and lungs. The water was unusually clear, and shafts of sun wavered down through it to play on the rippled sand. Amberjack and barracuda passed in and out of dark caverns in the cliff, the sunlight picking out intricate patterns on their backs. Fry drifted in layers of fine silver mesh, moving to an invisible pulse.

We dove deep down into the wet blue light, then hung suspended in a translucence so pure and perfect it evoked rapture. Lungs straining with our mortality, we drifted back through indigo and gold, shadow and light, and broke the calm surface for a long, sweet breath. We did it again and again for the sheer euphoria…and then we had to leave. The next day was Monday.

12.

OLD LUKE

Old Luke was a black Lab who lived on the Coral Bay dock. Day in and day out, he lay in the same spot, about halfway down its length. Through stinging winter squalls and blistering summer heat he was there, raising his head and giving a couple thumps with his tail to greet the first skiff to come ashore at dawn and bid goodnight to the last one off in the wee hours.

Nobody knew how old he was. The visiting vet, who took the ferry over from St. Thomas once a week, and treated him for free, guessed he must be 17, the equivalent of a hundred-plus in human years.

Old Luke looked it, gaunt, sway-backed, arthritic, with loose folds of skin hanging about his neck and jowls, and his mournful, clouded eyes peering out from deep in their sockets. When he had to move he would heave a reluctant sigh and lift himself with visible effort onto shaky legs and stand there for a moment steadying himself before moving off. Soon he'd be back to resume his vigil, his sad eyes always looking wistfully out to sea.

He was waiting for Andy, his master, to row up in his dinghy and tie it once again to the same rusted black iron cleat he had always used. The old dog waited patiently for years, becoming a fixture on the Coral Bay dock but he waited in vain. Andy was dead. At least, that's what everybody thought. His body was never found but one morning his sailboat was washed up in the surf at Drunk Bay where its shattered hulk lies today, high and dry on the exposed rock beach where hurricane swells eventually lifted it.

Andy had been a reclusive, grey-haired drifter with a face that had been battered by hard living. A skein of tiny red capillaries laced his nose; and his hands, normally clasped around a green Heineken bottle, shook slightly. He had sailed in with his dog one day on a battered old fiberglass sloop — and ended up staying for a year or so. Not many people got to know him, though. He mostly stayed on his boat and drank a bottle of rum a day, sometimes on a bad day, two. To his credit he wasn't a loud roaring drunk, determined to give the sleeping harbor the benefit of his drunken epiphanies — unlike some. He kept his boat apart, at the outer edge of the mooring area and rowed to shore with Luke always sitting in the bow, to buy supplies. So far as anyone could remember he never left the anchorage until the day he died.

That day he left the harbor under full sail, too late in the afternoon, headed for St. Croix, forty miles south. The passage between the islands can be rough and Andy's boat was not particularly seaworthy, but on this day it didn't matter because he never even made it out to the open sea.

It was Ram's Head that did for him.

Ram's Head is the southernmost tip of St. John, a great knob of rock at the end of a long, low peninsula that reaches far enough out into the Caribbean Sea to disturb the sweep of the oceanic swells that the trade winds have driven all the way from Africa.

Out on the deep ocean these waves are uniform and steady and roll harmlessly under a vessel's stern but once they enter the shelf of shallow water that bears the Virgin Islands they grow unsettled and confused. They sense the bottom rising and feel the shock waves rebounding from the wall of rock that lies ahead, death throes of their comrades before them. They end their free frolicking run across three thousand miles of open Atlantic in an ugly, violent mood, exploding in such a fury against Ram's Head's implacable rock that a hiker standing atop it can feel the vibrations of the impact.

Perhaps he missed his step in the steepened seas, the edge of his balance blunted by a long spell at anchor and too much rum. Perhaps he stepped over on purpose. But most likely he lost his grip on the rigging when he used both hands to unzip his fly. Falling overboard is the most common cause of accidental death at sea; and they say that most drowned men who have fallen off yachts are recovered — if they ever are — with their flies unzipped.

At any rate, his boat washed ashore at, appropriately, Drunk Bay, where white-shouldered ranks of rollers shattered it against the rock beach. The beach is a long gradual curve of smooth shiny rocks about the size of a fist that tumble over each other in the surf...nature's rock polisher.

The noise of that dense clattering, the rock rolling over and over, countless tons of granite in motion, may have been the last sound Andy heard on this earth as he drowned — if that's what happened. His body was never found.

Luke was found next to the wrecked hull, howling a woeful lament. Kind souls brought him back to Coral Bay where he colonized that spot on the dock, where Andy had always tied up his dinghy, and waited patiently, determined to be there when his master might arrive.

He was such a dear old soul, the epitome of a faithful dog that the boating community took him under their care. Several ladies who lived on boats made a point of remembering him when they had bones to dispose of; and there always seemed to be leftovers in his bowl. Sandy, the proprietress of the marine store at the head of the dock, made sure he had water, and Chutney her six-year-old daughter would occasionally sit with him and brush his coat, then give him a hug, her little blonde head laid against his neck. Only then would Luke forget his vigil for a moment, turn his anxious gaze from the harbor to give Chutney a touching look of gratitude, his ears back and a grimace of a smile on his face as he panted a little louder, before returning to his watch.

Then one day the good old heart cracked and at the cumbrous age of 18 he was gone. The next day someone had painted on the dock the outline of Luke's body in its usual position and written within it "Luke R.I.P." That image lasted a couple more years before the elements and people's feet wore it quite away.

By that time Andy the drifter had been mourned and remembered more than many a wealthy, sober man.

13.

BACKSTREET

Santos made few concessions to his size; but the fact remained that if it came to throwing his weight around he was inherently limited by his 11-pound mass. He just wasn't one of your 90-pound dogs. Santos got his results instead by a reliance on speed, agility... and bluff.

Santos was incredibly fast — and not just the sheer speed of a racecourse, but agile fast, quick. The sinews of his bandy little legs were strung with bow cord; he could instantly spring backwards or forwards or sideways, turn on a dime, feint and counter feint in the blink of an eye. This swift, deft rapier-like control was his main weapon — that and a histrionically vicious growl.

At East End Santos, after much practice, perfected the act and the art of guerrilla blitzkrieg, the equivalent of a jungle platoon impersonating a battalion — mostly smoke and mirrors, but convincing in the short run. His maniacal snarling projected the all-important psychological component, the threat that however small this animal, it was out of control, berserk. Coupled with his flat out charge — totally confidant, irrevocable as a bullet — the message was unmistakable — FEAR THIS!

An unforgettable example of this occurred the day I took Raff to interview for a place in the tenth-grade class of a private school in St. Thomas, because our St. John schools ended with

ninth grade. I had to bring Santos along — a hassle in the days
before car ferries because most taxis looked down their nose at
the prospect of a dog soiling their immaculate ride. Anyway we
tied him just inside the school gate and proceeded to the principal's office where we cooled our heels awhile, while she spoke
at length over the phone.

She finally received us, none too enthused at the idea of
Raffy entering the tenth-grade class after the school year had
begun. To make matters worse, he had been home schooled
for the past two years. She averred that he would have to do 9th
grade over to make sure he had an understanding of the basics.
Raffy reacted unhappily and I tried to explain that he wanted to
be with his age group.

"Oh no," she cut me off imperiously, "that's putting the
cart before the horse. First thing is to master the work...he will
be a little older than his classmates, but..."

"Ma'm he'll be almost two years older due to his birthday
falling late in the school year — socially that's a difficulty for a
teenager —!"

"Please...!" she fixed me with a look that must have brought
generations of young malefactors to their knees. It stopped me
cold. "Do...not...expect...me ...to lower the standards of my
School to meet your...your...I must inform you that I have
encountered this so called ...home schooling..." she pronounced
it like was a mouthful of sour milk, "and I have found this ...home
schooling ... to be invariably substandard. The class he wants to
join is very advanced and already full and I doubt there is room
even if he could meet the standards. At any rate he will have to
take our entrance exams — and that will be the final arbiter.
There's nothing more for you to say." She looked quite dour.

"OK," I said, and left Raffy to take the tests, telling him to
meet me down the street at a place we could get lunch. I untied
Santos from the gate and went to the marine store. On the way
back we found ourselves in the heart of Charlotte Amalie on
Back Street, a crowded one-way street congested with creeping
traffic with scant sidewalk space or none at all. Whereas Main
Street is all elegance (if you consider gift shops flogging booze

and useless but costly trinkets elegant), crowded with tourists and taxis and expectant merchants, Back Street by contrast is low rent, shops catering to locals, shops selling sports goods or African fashions, deep fry joints, and hole-in-the-wall rum shops.

We were walking close to the shop entrances, squeezed over by the traffic, Santos pulling on his leash, head down, dogged, breathing exhaust. This was definitely not his favorite place to be, and he was eager to get to the hillside park at the end of the street. We approached the entrance to a rum shop. A stoop and a doorway led into a narrow room, lined by a long counter and cheap barstools — the kind of place where voluptuous Spanish speaking women congregate towards dusk, still waking up, in sleazy shorts and half-buttoned blouses, the kind of place that features in the newspaper as the venue of a brawl or a stabbing late of nights.

This being only midafternoon, a group of rowdy but good-natured young West Indian men were firing shots of rum inside and lounging on the stoop drinking Guiness. You could see from their flushed countenances they were buzzed. When they saw Santos coming they started bantering, digging each other in the ribs, pointing at him and laughing, calling out comments.

"Me son....!? Wha da is? Walkin 'pon a leash like a dahg...buh da cyan' be no dahg!"

"Look like a pig!"

"A hedge hahg!"

"Yo schupid up! Dass a dahg yes!"

They appealed to me, "Mistah...dass a dahg fo true?"

"Yup," I answered. "He's a boat dog, bred to work on boats." I paused for a moment while they gazed at Santos, bemused, while Santos stared at the pavement, unamused, eager to be outa there. As we started to move on, one of the guys leaned down and pretended to grab at Santos' face, not in a mean way but just to get a reaction. Santos turned his head away and kept pulling. He wanted nothing to do with these noisy drunks seeking entertainment at his expense. The guy did it again, determined to have some fun, and once more the little dog flinched away — this time with a warning growl. But that only served to encourage the fellow and he feinted at Santos again.

This time without warning Santos went literally ballistic. With a bloodcurdling snarl he leaped up at the guy, a blur of speed that brought his audibly snapping teeth a millimeter from the offender's hand, crotch, thigh and ankle — all in a spectacular backwards arc that was an acrobatic tour de force.

The brother jerked back, tripped on the step and fell onto the stoop while his buddies exploded with laughter and cheered the dog. They were all on their feet, gesticulating at the dog to wait, come back, do it again, but with a smile I waved them off and we proceeded, Santos pulling like a sledge dog. We left them laughing and rhetorically augmenting the little dog's awesome aerial assault. We could still hear them going at it animatedly, halfway down the next block.

In a cafe opposite the park we met Raff. I asked him how he did.

"Alright, I guess. I like the school—the kids seem friendly — but I'm not going to do 9th grade again, dad."

"Don't worry, we'll work something out."

We returned at the appointed hour and were ushered in to the principal's office without delay. This time she put down her work and almost jumped to her feet. Gone was the dour visage. Her eyes beamed warmly as she extended her hand.

"Good to see you Mr. Muilenburg...and Rafael...Rafael," she purred his name. "You are a promising young man...yes indeed.... promising."

"How did he do?"

"Let us say...quite well."

"Well enough to get a place in the tenth grade? Because otherwise we'll have to go elsewhere."

"Oh no, not elsewhere...there will be a place for him here... I...Oh yes, you inquired about the possibility of a scholarship, on the application form — the financial aid committee has to meet but I think, ah, you can hope for a good outcome."

I couldn't resist asking, "So, his home schooling — not as bad as you feared?" But she ignored that and bustled about with Raffy, concentrating only on him.

When she noticed me again it was to say, "Ah, you may leave now so that we can proceed with Rafael's orientation."

She was a piece of work, that principal, but passionate about her school and her students. She focused her considerable persona on Raffy for the next three years. As it turned out, she knew what she was doing...the Raff didn't let her down.

14.

GALVANIZED IN PARADISE

It wasn't the best of circumstances for two gringo sailors —
a broken down truck, heavily loaded with anchors and chain, on
a lonely road in a deep Venezuelan forest inhabited by bandits
with a reputation for kidnap and murder. Night was closing in
fast. Manic vegetation choked everything but the asphalt, and
vines twined like pythons from the limbs of towering trees. The
clear bright Caribbean, so near, suddenly seemed so far away.

It had sounded like a great idea a week earlier as we drank
good Polar cerveza and watched the rain pour down on our
anchored boats. Tropical storm Joan was battering the offshore
islands of Los Roques and Tortuga but those of us sheltering at
Puerto Carenero on the mainland were snug in mud and mangroves, enjoying the spectacle from a pleasant seaside bar.
Conversation that afternoon went from weather to anchors to
chain vs. rope and then spawned an idea. All of us had rusty
chain and anchors that even as we watched were bleeding down
our boats' topsides. Only three hours away by truck was a galvanizing plant in the boondocks that did good work very reasonably — the Venezuelan bolivar had been tumbling steadily
against the US dollar. If we jointly hired a truck we could transport our ground tackle directly to the factory and back — quick,
cheap, straightforward.

In the event it was cheap; but straightforward? Well...more

like very interesting. It sure was real different from loading a U-haul and driving it down the interstate to an industrial park on the outskirts of Seattle.

But then Venezuela is supposed to be different. That's why we were there. Where else can one dive on mile after mile of off-shore reef in gin-clear water, or watch flocks of parrots and scar-let ibis settle into mangroves at sunset, or gaze at coastal sierras that soar from the sea to 9000 feet?

But the differences didn't stop there. The society is different too, operating on a set of premises that incorporate "manana," bribery — even bandits. We got more than our anchor gear gal-vanized — we got our psyches hot-dipped in third world reality.

It was a leap of faith to begin with. Amazing stories circu-lated among the beach bars about the local galvanizing estab-lishments. One place cut up a 100-meter length of anchor chain into ten meter pieces, then galvanized it and wondered why the owner had a fit when they had, at no extra charge, simpli-fied his life. The furnace at another factory broke down and when the sailor came to pick up his gear he was shown a five-ton block of zinc. His anchors were in there. Repair parts for the furnace had been ordered from Italy but were lost in the mail and not really expected for another three months, so if he were in a hurry they'd lend him a blowtorch.

Our outfit had a good track record. They had done an excellent job on my Danforth the year before. This time the Caracas office said that big jobs like a lot of chain would have to be brought to the factory. They gave me a map to find it in a small industrial town by a river in the interior, and a note to the factory manager that would command high priority.

Shel was skeptical. An ex-Navy man and retired TV news exec, Shel was bluff and bald, with a voice you could hear through thunder, and a tongue permanently in cheek. He weighed his choices bluntly. With a lot of chain and a couple of big anchors, he was inclined to wait til he got to Puerto La Cruz where a Venezuelan agent would have it done, but for twice the price. More expensive but probably more reliable, he boomed, cocking his eye at me, who was to be unpaid agent by virtue of having proposed the idea and speaking emergency Spanish.

On the other hand, his buddy in Puerto La Cruz had consigned his tackle to an agent, and one-week delivery had turned into two going on three and still no sign of the goods. The tropical storm passing to the north had given him a bad night hanging to only one anchor. Shel finally decided to throw his lot in with us and got in touch with his friend the next morning via ham radio to tell him he'd found a much better deal, half the price, no waiting, an inside job. His buddy predicted disaster.

Early on the appointed morning we converged on the dock. Shel brought "Rainbow" alongside, while the rest of us ferried our loads ashore in dinghies almost awash with the weight of rusty iron. Counting ten anchors, a thousand-plus feet of assorted chain, and fittings, it must have weighed two tons.

With everything in a heap we awaited the truck. One of the dockworkers had sworn his cousin would be there before 9 a.m. with his vehicle. At 9:30 a search of the premises revealed that our middleman had disappeared. At 10 o'clock still no truck. It was getting hot on the dock and Shel was mopping his brow and rumbling quaint aphorisms picked up years ago in the Navy. Word finally came that our man and his cousin had decided to visit friends in the country instead.

There was nothing for it but to hop a jitney into town, get out at the first likely truck, and walk around it, kicking tires. Right away the owner appeared, scowling suspiciously in a shop doorway. Five minutes later we had a deal and were on our way back to the dock, where the chain gang loaded, and kissed goodbye, all its ground tackle.

The truck bed was rusted through but the engine was strong. The first hour took us past lush plantations and well watered pastures where huge mango trees shaded the roadside and breadfruits stood over every dwelling. Peasants watched us go by from their doorsteps. Fernando, our driver, handled his truck like Ben-Hur in the chariot race. He careened through villages, scattered chickens, and fishtailed around curves, all the while apologizing that the heavy load ruined his truck's cornering.

The next hour found us climbing high into the beautiful hills of the Guatopo National Park. We passed waterfalls and cascades of orchids, and looked out over range after range of luxuriantly forested mountains, an endless canopy of treetops carpeted in flowers and butterflies and glossy creepers.

Fernando's rapid fire Spanish went in one ear and out the other, but one word suddenly stuck with a quiver — "bandidos." We had him run it by us again, slowly, and learned that bandit guerrillas roamed the jungle with impunity. During the day we were safe, but at night they would cut trees down across the road and rob vehicles, sometimes kidnapping for ransom or killing the occupants. Nobody cared to come through after dark.

"Nobody?" I asked. "What about the police?"

"Especially not the police!" Fernando laughed. "The bandidos want their weapons." He gave a waggish look while he sawed at his throat with his finger.

We arrived at Santa Theresa del Tuy, a small industrial town sprawled in ramshackle inelegance by a brown river. A rutted dirt track that made Fernando curse led to the factory — a large tin roof covering some machinery, a small office, and a long vat emitting evil fumes.

The floor boss came up, listened, looked at our stuff, and shook his head almost scornfully. Three weeks minimum before he could touch it. He waved his hand at a pile of anchor gear on the ground, which I'd already noticed with misgivings, and at a backlog of rusty girders that were stacked by the hundreds out in the yard. "ImposSEEblay!" Case closed.

I produced my ace in the hole, the note from the Caracas headquarters, and asked stiffly for the factory manager. With obvious satisfaction, the floor boss informed me that the jefe was very sick and hadn't been to work for two weeks. Things were looking bad when a slim young man walked up, immaculately dressed, pencil moustache, carrying a slide rule — the plant engineer. He looked intelligent, spoke good English, and listened to our story with sympathy. After I finished he reflected for a moment and then said, three days. We thanked him and drove back to Carenero feeling relieved. Shel conveyed the tidings that evening to his buddy who predicted three months, maybe three weeks, but three days? No way Jose!

Friday morning we looked for Fernando's arrival at 8 a.m. in vain. We went into town and found him at the body shop, working with a welder. Sparks were flying. The truck's bed was gone and they were fabricating a new one. Fernando looked blank when we reminded him about our appointment, but rallied and sent a small boy off with a message. Soon Enrique drove up in a vintage Chevy truck, we struck a bargain, and left.

This time Bill came along. Dressed in yachting attire — cutoffs, T-shirt and flip-flops — he was an ex-hippy with graying hair, a kind face, and an easy manner. He and his wife had sold their California farm to developers, bought a 34-foot sloop, and gone cruising. He had some chain and an anchor in the deal and wanted to see some of the country.

When we passed through the forest Enrique started talking about the bandidos but we had no problem til we came to the outskirts of the town and ran into a roadblock. Not bandits per se, but the police.

When our turn came the officer demanded ID. Enrique had his ready, I produced my passport, and Bill, with a weak grin, offered a tattered scrap that had once been a draft card. The cop wrinkled his nose and wouldn't touch it. His scathing remarks passed over our heads, but from his look of grim satisfaction it was clear he wasn't about to let the matter drop — no more than a hungry cat would release a plump mouse out of pity. This was dinner.

"It's just as well I didn't bring my passport," Bill told me from the corner of his mouth. "We still haven't cleared in to the country yet."

Hadn't cleared in? Super! I began to review what I really knew about Bill, but then he explained, while the cop and Enrique conferred in the shade of a nearby tree. Bill and his wife had been beating up the Caribbean coast of South America all the way from Panama. Going against stiff winds and a current running sometimes 2 knots against them, they'd experienced their full share of the miseries for which that route is notorious. On leaving Curacao however, they caught a lucky wind out of the north and rode it nonstop to the east, only putting in to Carenero because of tropical storm Joan. Then this galvanizing deal came up. As I said, he was a laid-back kind of guy, but getting less so by the minute.

The policeman told Bill he would have to face the judge. No passport...serious offense in Venezuela...and since it was now Friday the hearing wouldn't be held til Monday. What were we supposed to do in the meantime, I asked. He shrugged, supremely unconcerned. Enrique and I were free to go, but Bill would have to wait in jail.

After this ultimatum he walked off a few yards. He didn't pull Bill out of the car and he didn't call a paddy wagon. The glimmer of his game began to show. Enrique gave a sardonic smile and rubbed his thumb back and forth over his fingertips.

Of course...what else? I pulled a 100-bolivar note out from the kitty, about $3, and Enrique took it to the cop, gesticulating elaborately as he spoke. They came back, the policeman talking truculently about the judge and the immutable course of justice. Enrique said to me, "Not enough." I peeled off another one and the two of them conferred again, then returned. The cop looked like a man to double business bound. "Very irregular...I could get into trouble..." Another 50 bolivars, I gave it to him direct, and he waved us on and resumed his post in the shakedown. The immutable object, justice, had met the irresistible force; in this case about $7.50 US, and folks, we had a winner!

Lest this sounds cynical, recall that the Spaniards cut their way to power here, then sold public office to the highest bidder, who was expected to use the powers of his office to recoup his investment, with a profit. Ever since, many public jobs are not only a meager salary, but also a license to collect certain bribes. So, if one is guilty of a minor infraction, and the cop is decent enough, why not pay him direct instead of hassling with courts, judges and fines that may well line the pocket of someone far less needy than a provincial flatfoot?

The factory had done beautiful work. Everything was double-dipped and bright with zinc. We loaded the truck, got waved through the roadblock, and entered the hills of the Guatopo forest late in the afternoon. As we climbed the steep grades it became apparent that Enrique's truck had nowhere near the power of Fernando's. We crept upwards at a painfully slow rate, the engine about to have a hernia. It started to cough, lost power, and stalled.

Enrique got out and lifted the hood. The radiator was steaming. He looked at it somberly, and then glanced over his shoulder at the dense woods. I remembered the bandits and wished we had something valuable for them to steal. The idea of them dragging off 100 meters of ½-inch chain up the jungle slopes was comical — but the bandits might not laugh.

Enrique took a jug to one of the many rivulets that streamed down the hill and filled the radiator with cool water, slowly, at Bill's warning, so as not to crack the block. Ten minutes later the truck started up out of its coma and plodded uphill a little farther. Rigid in our seats, we willed the old girl on with bated breath, but soon she began to wheeze. She shuddered violently and gave up the ghost.

We came to rest overlooking a steep gorge where a long waterfall poured down past yellow blossoms whose petals glistened with droplets. The trees were gigantic, the view superb, but the light was fading and we had a problem. Even if we were spared the bandits, what kind of miserable night would we spend in a dank jungle on a godforsaken road? Only one car had come by so far and when we tried to flag it down the driver had gunned the accelerator and shot through with a fixed glare that said "not a chance, fella!"

Off trudged Enrique once again to fill the jug. I noticed a fallen tree at the side of the road and shards of glass beside it...ominous portent.

Meanwhile Bill was deep inside the hood, talking to himself. "Enrique is a good ol' boy but he don't know much about trucks. I used to have one of these old Chevys on the farm...she should be makin' this grade. Maybe the carburetion is off...what with the altitude, and this load...hmmm." He pulled out an omni-bladed Swiss army knife, extended the screwdriver and started fiddling with the carburetor. Enrique and I watched him hopefully.

"OK, start her up," he said, and so help me, she roared to life when Enrique turned the key. Pebbles shot out from the rear tires as we pulled off the shoulder. It was still a strain getting that load up and over the divide, but she made it and we coasted back down to the lowlands whistling Dixie. It was pitch black by the time we left the forest behind.

Cheers and beers greeted us back at the dock where we unloaded the truck by moonlight and flashlight. When everything had been sorted out I was rowing past Shel's boat and could hear him on the ham to his buddy who was anxious to know how we had fared. Shel was working him over good.

"Yeah, our stuff got top priority...a bunch of other chain been rusting up there for weeks, big backlog...that's what he said...I hear you, no need to shout, Hal...what can I tell you? Ours took three days flat and cost a fraction of that.... nah, probably just ran out of zinc...miners' strike...not to worry Hal, they have to arbitrate next month..."

15.

JOY AND GRIEF ON THE LAS AVES REEF

The wind's firm hand drove Breath's bow through the sea like a stylus, wedging up a white wake that tumbled past and sighed behind her, as moment by moment the little scrap of land ahead grew more distinct. When we were close enough to see individual rocks on the strand, we turned and ran down the coastal drop-off, where sun-drenched shallows of the shore fell off into the abyss, as purple as old port.

Our two boys drank it all in eagerly. They'd never been here but for years they'd heard the story of the wreck of the French flotilla, and they'd dreamed of finding treasure here on the Las Aves reef.

One of the great blunders in Caribbean naval history took place on a windy night in 1678 when a flotilla of French warships, sent to capture Curacao from the Dutch, instead piled up on a deadly reef. In a classic case of crossed signals, the first ship to crack its back against the coral sounded off warning guns. Being less than a day's sail from their target, the rest of the fleet assumed the canny Hollanders had somehow managed to ambush their van. Hastily they ran out their guns, beat to quarters—and smartly sailed into the breakers.

They wrecked on the reef of Las Aves de Sotovento, an atoll in the south Caribbean. At the time, with the death of 500 men, the loss of a fleet and the counterattack of the Dutch, there could have been little doubt where this debacle took place. But over the centuries, confusion arose because Las Aves de Sotovento was unknown, so insignificant it didn't even warrant a name on most maps. Aves (Bird) Island, on the other hand, an even smaller speck in the northeast Caribbean, was a notorious and well-charted hazard to navigation, a lethal spider in the center of a web of well-traversed shipping routes.

Donald Street, the author of the definitive Caribbean cruising guide, assumed Aves Island was the place and noted that some eighteen ships wrecked in such close proximity should have left ample debris on the sea floor, yet divers found no trace of the disaster. It was a great mystery, and of more than academic interest — the admiral's flagship would have carried chests of silver coins — operating funds. A fortune lay somewhere in the shallow water.

In the mid-1970's, while cruising single-handed along the north rim of South America, I stopped at Aves de Sotovento. The Guardia Frontera post, a tiny building underneath a huge Venezuelan flag baked, somnolent, under the brilliant sun. At the rattle of my anchor chain, a man appeared in the doorway, jumped into a big zodiac, and gunned it out to my boat. He looked wild, his long black hair whipping in the wind, his skin burned dark by the sun, his swimsuit his entire uniform. There was an almost desperate air about him.

I handed him my ship's papers. He waved them away impatiently, gave me a piercing look and asked, "Do you smoke?"

"No," I replied. His face crashed.

"I do have some cigarettes, though..." I kept a couple of cartons aboard for barter, so I gave him a pack. He lit one up with trembling hands and an ease spread over his features. We talked and he told me his story.

For many years stationed in the dense jungles near Venezuela's border with Brazil, he eventually made the mistake of snorting the hallucinogenic drug the Indians called "yopo." It drove him mad, he said. Fearing the Indians might kill him, terrified of the gloomy, wet forest, he obtained a transfer to Las Aves, the brightest, driest, most open posting in the country. He'd been there for two years, snorkeling the great reef, and his only complaint was when the monthly supply vessel skipped a visit and he ran out of cigarettes.

When I came ashore I brought him the rest of the carton. He was overcome with gratitude. "How can I repay you, amigo?"

"Take me to some good snorkeling?" I struck a chord there.

The next morning, we sped in the Zodiac out to the barrier reef that stretched ten miles north from the end of the island. He took some pains to find the precise place — and when we went over the side the first thing I saw, in fifteen feet of crystal clear water, was bronze cannons lying in a heap and a big old anchor with a delicate fan of fire coral growing two feet high on its shank. He beckoned me to follow a short distance and lo! There was another wreck, and another. Eventually I counted six such clumps of guns and anchors.

I suddenly remembered the name of this place on the detailed chart — Las Aves de Sotovento. This was the Aves the French had wrecked on, not the Isla de Aves. It made sense now. This reef was less than a day's sail from Curacao — and subject to strong, unpredictable currents.

When I noticed a rim of metal in the sand and dug out a bronze ship's bell, I remember thinking that this might be the high point of my snorkeling career. Back in the Zodiac I gazed in rapture at the best thing I'd ever found, then said reluctantly, "I guess this belongs in the museum in Caracas?"

He looked at me quizzically. "You like it?" I nodded emphatically. "You keep it. The museum have plenty!" My delight made him smile — the bell easily trumped the Marlboros. When we left, I mentally gauged the distance to an old freighter impaled upright on the reef and vowed to return.

It took me many years — so much of life intervened — but at last I had come back, this time with my wife and two sons who could dive like otters, in the boat we'd built ourselves. The bell, talisman of the great reef, was proudly mounted on our mainmast. The admiral's chest of silver flitted through our minds...

We finally came to anchor in placid water behind the great Las Aves reef, which stretched in a great horseshoe arc as far as we could see in both directions. What a glorious anchorage! No land broke the perfect circle of the horizon, so we could lie on the deck and gaze at fully half the universe overhead. The lagoon shimmered aquamarine. And not another boat was in sight — except for the handful of stranded ships including the old freighter, my reference mark.

The next morning, we began our search. The weather was light, perfect for taking the skiff safely through to the outside reef. At what I judged to be the right distance from the freighter we entered the water. With our ears, nose and mouth stopped, beauty exploded in through our eyes.

Enormous brain corals were hedged about by thickets of richly textured gold elk horn. A four-eyed butterfly fish emerged from a cave into a shaft of sunshine that lit its fins with a yellow flame so pure and intense I can see it still. A carpet of small snappers, thousands of them, blanketed the floor; while drifts of tiny silversides, hung amidst the coral branches like a gauzy lace veil, flashed in the swell, making visible the invisible pulse of the sea.

Wrecks and wreckage were not hard to find. We saw a big iron cylinder, all riveted and bolted, perhaps part of a steam engine, and farther down a section of hull with the ribs showing. We swam over the wreck of an old schooner, her bowsprit and cutwater intact, at her stern a graceful quarter moon rudder. She lay head to the reef and must have been under full sail when she struck, like an arrow into oak.

For three days we combed the reef, swimming in formation, each person within sight of the next, from shallow to deep so that we could scan a wide swathe. The wreckage would have to be within that zone. As we drifted in the clear water, the only swimmers in a thousand square miles of sea, we saw wonderful sights — a jewfish, huge, under a hollowed-out coral head like a lion under a tree on the African savannah — a shark, coalescing out of the blue like a ghost coming through a wall, taking a form most palpable, that passed insouciantly by, then dematerialized just as it had come. But we didn't see the wrecks of the French flotilla...no guns, no coins.

And now the weather was changing, getting gustier, with more wind and dark skirted squalls riding a slate-colored sea. We would have to leave — without finding the wrecks.

Had I imagined it all, so many years ago? But there was the bell. Perhaps I had just misjudged the location, or someone had salvaged them, or hurricane swells had buried them. Our last day there we took the skiff along the inside of the reef to explore an inter-island trader which had quite recently plowed straight onto the reef. Its keel had carved a long trench in the coral, exposing two big cannons, which must have been buried for 250 years!

So the great reef had its secrets still. God only knew what lay beneath the coral, what riches, what tragedies. We sailed off well satisfied. As for the admiral's chest of silver, our family had the coinage of our memories, whose interest the years would surely compound. And I still had the bronze bell, more precious to me than any bar of gold.

16.

AZORES HIGH

In the morning of our 23rd day at sea, we got our first glimpse of land. Ilheu do Pico's 8000-foot cone stood lavender blue in the distance, an unwavering mark amidst the dissembling clouds gathered on the horizon

All day, Pico drew us like a magnet. As we closed with the Azores we watched it grow, dominating its surroundings. Even after we'd reached safe harbor in neighboring Faial, Pico lay just across a narrow channel, still commanding attention. Rich with refraction, the late afternoon sunlight came slanting off the sea and embossed a patina of delicate gold on the soaring rocky peak. It looked like an altar held high to heaven.

We couldn't set sail from the Azores without first setting foot on Pico.

Hence, one glorious summer morning we took the earliest ferry across to Pico, and boarded a bus for the far end of the island. It wound along narrow roads whose embankments blazed with masses of primrose and hydrangea. We passed stone walled fields and orchards, little towns all clustered around a church, fishing villages perched safely above the blue sea, and ubiquitous latticed grape vines protected from the wind behind low walls of black pumice stone. But everywhere on Pico the prime sight, the inevitable backdrop to every view...was the mesmerizing rise of rock, the great peak.

When, at lunch, we learned from backpackers that a steaming vent at the crater had kept them warm all night. I decided then and there to climb the peak with my 12-year-old son, and spend the night there — this very day. The weather was perfect — exceptionally clear and warm and predicted to remain that way. We'd been handed an opportunity.

Twelve hours later we would be sorely wishing we had asked more about the vent.

A taxi took us to the trailhead, first stopping at the driver's home to dig out a large sheet of polyethylene plastic. I declined the unsolicited gift, citing the warm vent; a troubled look crossed his face — I had little Portuguese and he little English — but he gauged our clothing dubiously (jeans, T-shirts and light windbreakers) and pressed it into my hands; so I stuffed it in my pack.

We started off in trees and greenery at about 3,000 feet. The path didn't waste time zigzagging; it went straight uphill and soon emerged into scrubby, unmistakably volcanic terrain, with occasional conical vents jutting from the lower slopes and the now cold and hollow shells of what once were downhill running rills of hot lava rock. The trail got progressively rockier and steep, the air more pure, the view more spectacular. After a couple of hours we were looking down at the mile-high mountaintops of Faial.

Eventually all signs of a trail disappeared on the impervious stone and we had to find our own way to the top. We gradually made the transition from hiking to rock climbing, using our hands as much as our feet. The ascent was exhilarating, working our way up steep faces, not looking out and across to similarly elevated peaks — but looking down, dizzyingly down, all the spiraling way down to the sea.

Wonderful — but also taking much more time than we had anticipated. It was getting late as we reached the top and climbed over the wall of the crater's rim and made our way down to its incredibly rugged floor — a bleak, nightmarish spot — crater walls surrounding a gravel floor that was strewn with boulders big and little, with tortured outcroppings and no sign of anything more sentient than a lichen — and no indication of a warm vent.

© Don E. Brown 2004

We picked our way through the silent maze of boulders to the opposite side of the crater where the rim had broken off flush with the crater floor. When I cautiously approached to look over the side, a shock wave of vertigo hammered me back. It was like looking out the open door of a plane. A sheer drop went down 3,000 feet straight as a plumb bob. If you jumped or slipped you would freefall three-fifths of a mile before hitting so much as a twig. It was a stunning sight.

But the sun was nearing the horizon and we still hadn't found the vent. At the highest part of the rim a dwarf cone about 200 feet high jutted like a nipple into the sky. That now was the only candidate for the steaming vent, but the ascent looked slippery — downright dangerous — in the fast failing light. And if we got to the top and there was no vent — then what? Stuck all night clinging to the most exposed crag between New Hampshire and the Alps?

We had arrived too late.

On the floor of the crater a few crude shelters of rock had been built maybe 400 years ago for lookouts when enemy fleets cruised the islands. They were the only shelter in sight, extensions of natural caves and crevices. They looked like crude Stone Age coffins and they promised a miserably cold and dank place to spend the night. We picked one that we could both just fit in. At least its floor wasn't wet. So be it.

We stayed outside watching the sunset, an incredibly pure affair with the earth visibly turning as gauged by the sun steadily sinking below the horizon, leaving a pool of molten orange on the western sea, while aloft gold and lavender afterglow burned and faded high in the sky. Up here the colors were honed to their essence without the garish filter of the atmosphere at sea level. The air in our lungs tingled. Soon the stars were out, cold and brilliant as polished ice.

The temperature dropped drastically after the sun went down and the wind came up. We gladly climbed into the entrance of our sarcophagus, scarcely room to even kneel. and spread out the plastic over the uneven stone — a miserable excuse for a bed, but at least we were out of the wind. With a flashlight for lighting we had supper — a hunk of cheese, some bread, and half a bottle of red wine.

Eventually we huddled together and tried to sleep. The rock chafed at our hips and shoulders. The cold of the primeval mountain leeched the warmth out of our bones. After a while the moisture of our breathing condensed on the stone roof just above us and it started to drip. We turned on the flashlight and this time apportioned the plastic as part ground cover, part protective blanket. We drifted off to fitful sleep, teeth chattering helplessly. Sometime before dawn I fumbled for the flashlight and looked at my watch: 11 p.m. . . . not even midnight.

Diego had occasionally suffered from bronchitis. I started to worry about him. He was shivering steadily. I gave him my outer shirt and he drifted off to sleep again while I tossed and turned, impossible to get comfortable, longing for the dawn. After an eternity between doze and wake I got up to look around outside and was knifed by the wind. Yet the sky remained clear, in fact extremely clear. The stars were incredible, hanging almost within reach, Jupiter huge, Scorpio emblazoned across the sky like a "connect the dots" drawing made for baby Jesus. I looked at my watch — minutes before one — and despaired of the dawn.

At 2 a.m. Diego started to shiver uncontrollably, and cough. His face felt feverish. I felt helpless. Had I laid my precious child on this cruel stone altar as a sacrifice to…what? The ionosphere? I wrapped my arms and my legs around his body and started rubbing his back vigorously, then his legs, slapping, kneading. After about an hour the coughing subsided and he fell into fitful sleep. Eventually I dozed off too, my feet like blocks of ice, my bones aching.

With the first intimation of dawn we got on the move. The stars were still intense, the wind cold, the sky, if possible, clearer.

Night turned to light, by stages gloomy, then gray, then grainy, then each moment brighter as its source approached the horizon and we climbed up the rim of the crater.

Here, at the top of the visible world, the sun started edging its rim over the horizon. We looked directly at it as more and more of it lifted itself into this world. I'd seen it bigger at sea level but up here it seemed refined by its fires into a hard pure orb of light. It shone like a buffed and polished copper gong.

The sun seemed to hang there for a moment, shedding the sea, still cool, still accessible to the naked eye. The first shafts of sunshine landed on our clothes, our faces. On that mountaintop I suddenly understood early man's worship of the sun. The majesty of the ancient God revealed itself in a blinding fire that first struck its crown and then flared down its countenance — an unbearable brilliance from which human eyes had to look away, unable to behold the face of God.

Then we saw the most marvelous sight I ever saw or probably ever will see. The sun, in the first moments of its blaze, on a day of the utmost clarity, without the slightest shred of cloud in the sky, sent a flood of radiance parallel across the surface of the ocean. It cast the shadow of the preternaturally perfect cone of Pico far as the eye could see. The lines of this huge cone lay across the channel, put half of Faial in shade, leaving the other half bright, then shadowed the ocean as far as the horizon, some hundred miles, and then forever out to space — where it travels yet at the speed of light.

The magnitude of it, the huge shadow — I'll never forget the cosmos at its infinite geometry.

We stood there watching it for about fifteen minutes, awestruck. Then the wind whipped at our shirts.

"Let's go, I'm cold," said Diego.

The descent was no easier than the ascent; if anything we were more likely to slip. Hands and feet, hands and feet, we gripped the cold crag and inched our way down, still exposed to the wind.

We climbed down for about an hour til we crossed a ridge and saw a few hundred yards below us a tiny valley sheltered from the wind, glowing in the morning sun. Here thickets of ancient dwarfed shrubs interlaced their gnarled branches to form a springy canopy of dense foliage three feet off the ground. They looked sturdy enough to bear our weight so we cautiously tried lying back and found it a perfect mattress. With almost a sob of gratitude we let go every aching muscle and lay there smelling the pungent branches and sweet wild flowers, hearing the comforting sound of the bees making their busy summer morning rounds.

We both fell asleep and dreamed of ambrosia and when we awoke it was time to get down the mountain to the road, hike buoyantly the long easy downhill slant til a farmer gave us a ride in his old pickup to where we could catch a taxi to the port and board the ferry for Horta and run laughing to the marina where we burst in upon the boat exclaiming our love of the mountain, God, and the Azores.

17.

TROPICAL WEATHER REPORT

Done it again! said the little voice.

Boxed yourself into a corner. Told everyone your plans. Now you have to perform — or look the fool. And this voyage! Sailing all the way to Africa for a cargo of, what — gourds? Pathetic. Don Quixote afloat!

At a quiet cove near St. John our 42-foot gaff ketch tugged at her anchor like a restless horse. Everything was ready — fuel, water, stores, new headsails — to sail across the North Atlantic via the Azores, Portugal and the Canaries, to West Africa. There we planned to pick up a cargo of calabashes, beautifully marked and endlessly useful native containers, to sell back in the Virgins.

But by now it was the second week of July in what was cheerily predicted to be the worst hurricane season in years; already two tropical storms had formed in June and just three days away from us was a strong, well-organized tropical wave.

Now I wasn't so keen to leave.

Back in March it had seemed a good enough plan. After all, I reasoned, July was still early in hurricane season — nothing happens before August. Should be simple; wait for the window of good weather between tropical waves, set sail on the heels of one and be 500 miles north by the time the next wave arrived — well above it, and any chance of its developing. With every succeeding day we'd be farther away from the hurricane zone.

It would be sheer bad luck to encounter a hurricane right then and there, and bad luck can just as easily find you crossing the street.

The problem was we couldn't leave the Caribbean til early July; it was either go then or not go at all. So we decided to roll with the odds — though the little voice had warned me that I would feel remarkably less carefree about it when July rolled around and the marine stores started to advertise specials on ground tackle and distribute free hurricane plotting charts.

I'd called the National Hurricane Center in Miami earlier that afternoon to ask about the oncoming tropical wave. You could tell the meteorologist on duty loved his work. "A beauty," he enthused. "Classic upper level formations...really well organized...more likely to see some action out of this baby than anything so far this season."

Just what I wanted to hear.

But on the other hand we had three days before the wave would arrive and the wind was good for going north in a hurry. If we holed up and waited for this "classic" to pass we'd just have to deal with another — satellite pictures showed a series of waves stacked up all the way to the Cape Verdes. Every day's delay was a day deeper into hurricane season. Plus, we'd said all our goodbyes, and to come limping back now...

So, we left. As dusk fell I took a long look at Jost Van Dyke, the last land before Bermuda. Ahead darkness settled over the uncontrollable immensity of the sea. I told myself we could still turn back tomorrow if the wave started to intensify or track more to the north, but the reassurance rang hollow. The die was cast.

A day later, when we theoretically could have turned back and made shelter before it arrived, the wave remained unchanged — "strong," favorable for development, but showing no signs of doing so. We had been averaging 7 knots to the N, and since it was continuing to head due W at 17 knots it should pass handily beneath us. So we pressed on.

The next morning, just past the point of no return, we tuned in NMN for the High Seas forecast and heard that the wave had intensified overnight. It was now "very strong" and aircraft reconnaissance reported squalls packing 35 to 40 knots — a tropical depression except for closed circulation of the winds. That was rectified by the following broadcast when it became official — a proper tropical depression with regular Coast Guard advisories and reconnaissance flights, and its inclusion in marine weather bulletins from Barbados to Boston.

But what really gave me pause were its revised coordinates; they had jumped a full degree farther north — the system was slowing down and veering more to the NW, that is, more towards us.

Ominous. It was supposed to go due west, and the faster the better, like they always do...well, almost always. I got the first glimmer of what was going to become a painfully bright light in the days to come — the uneasy awareness that things weren't going the way the pilot charts promised, the way they were supposed to.

On the Antilles net everyone was discussing where they were going to hole up. One boat was safe in Leinster Bay and the image of that snug anchorage surrounded by high green hills made me acutely homesick. But there was no turning back now. We had to run.

We had been heading almost due north with eased sheets, hurtling along on an ample close reach, riding force 6 easterly trades, to put as much distance as possible between us and the approaching wave. Now the same strategy required that we go close-hauled to keep at right angles to the storm's new NW course. What had been an exhilarating sail turned into a violent beat, with the boat bucking on its side. We needed both hands to move around the interior.

With the radically increased angle of heel, a nauseating, headachy odor began to faintly percolate through the cabin. It got steadily stronger...the unmistakable smell of diesel. Finally we found the leak — the vent hose just above the tank was spewing out a little jet of fuel, like a cherub in a fountain, every time the boat took a sharp roll.

That repaired and cleaned up, I returned to surfing the weather broadcasts, switching from the Coast Guard, to VI radio, to WWV and the various nets at all hours of the day and night, hoping to hear that the storm had dissipated, or sped up and hurtled below us to the west.

Instead it slowed down until it stalled, then intensified into a tropical storm. Now it got a name, Chantal. The flat computerized voice added that it was expected to become a full-fledged hurricane within 24 hours.

Stalled storms are dangerously unpredictable. With no momentum or sense of direction they often start moving in an unexpected way. I prayed for Chantal to fling herself into a Florida swamp, or to fulfil her destiny in the Arctic, selflessly obliterating herself to rectify the globe's temperature imbalance; but she bided her time — and kept intensifying.

As she intensified she expanded, til gale force winds extended 250 miles from her center, bringing her area of disturbed weather uncomfortably close to our position. That afternoon on Diego's watch a thick bank of heavy clouds rolled in low over the sea. Were we about to be enveloped by outlying squalls of the dangerous semi-circle, whose inward spiraling winds would drive us towards the storm center?

One of the thunderheads quivered with lightning. Awe-inspiring by night, by daylight the flashes were livid and sickly, a concealed evil like the flickering tongue of a serpent. Then came the wind, racing over the water, rasping up whitecaps almost phosphorescent in the dim light below the saturated underbelly of the nimbus. It struck the rig a blow; the boat lurched to her knees, and then took off — a 20-ton projectile tearing foam off the sea, til we dropped the main.

But soon the squall was past and the rest of the clouds brought merely a moist fresh breeze that died as the bank rolled ponderously on. By dark we had turned on the engine to make all possible speed away from the distant flashes that marked the storm's progress beyond the western horizon.

When the Coast Guard gave its extended outlook they warned that the predicted coordinates should be used "for guidance purposes only. Errors may be large." And so they were. Instead of paralleling the US east coast and brushing the Georges Banks as first predicted, the storm recurved sharply and did an arc around our position. We were OK, the weather was good, but always we were on tenterhooks being so close to an erratic storm that kept dogging us.

My brash assumptions about the average hurricane track had forgotten that "average" presupposes the existence of extremes. My eyes kept being drawn to the unusual track of a hurricane on my June pilot chart that recurved in an unheard of direction — SE — then did a tight loop-de-loop just west of Bermuda. If a storm could do that it could do anything. Another chart showed a track that churned straight up through the central Atlantic to the Azores. I had seen these tracks before but dismissed them as freaks. It occurred to me now that "freak" was a word habitually linked with weather. It was a description, a warning — not a write-off. The pilot chart used the proper word, "notable" storms.

I remember sitting at my chart table hunched over the radio and the pilot charts hearing once again that the storm had turned closer towards us and would be upgraded to hurricane intensity by 1400 hrs. The mechanical voice droned on... "seas to 24 feet, winds gusting to 80 knots, zone of 50 knot winds extending out 70 miles, numerous heavy thunderstorms and squalls with gale force winds...." The irrevocable reality of being out there with an erratic storm hit me like a brick — no possible refuge! How could I have put my family in this spot?

An old friend liked to sum up life in two words: NO GUARANTEES. We forget that on land, sometimes, benumbed and beguiled as we are by government programs, medical advances and legal redress. There must be a cure. It must be somebody's fault. Somebody has to pay. A remedy for every malady, a safety net for every slip.

But for us the only recourse was our own — keep sailing at right angles to the storm's course. As it headed NW we headed NE; as it headed N we headed E, aided by a southeasterly breeze. And as it veered sharply NE we went SE under power since the weather had turned clear and calm with a large, steep swell.

Eventually we got our wish — after we learned our lesson. Chantal finally passed N of us and, released from our orbit, shot off to cold seas at 31 knots, a banshee hell-bent for the Arctic. The National Hurricane Center issued its last advisory and Chantal passed into history.

As the storm passed by the weather became extremely clear. We could see a hundred miles past the horizon, to majestic banks of cloud whose fleecy white tops towered over the curve of the earth. That night may have been the loveliest there ever was. Above us half the universe went on forever, lit by distant galaxies, while down on the surface of the sea we cut the dark water like an iridescent knife, riding the swell from an expired storm, even as we steered toward the light of what, for all we knew, was a long dead star.

18.

METHUSELAH MEETS HOTSPUR

On a clear, calm day, midway between Bermuda and the Azores, I turned 50. Half a century is a milestone in anyone's life and I wanted to celebrate mine at sea, isolated from the distracting swirl of life ashore, with time and space to digest my two score and ten. But, truth be told, the real reason for being at sea in my own boat was a fairly obvious gesture of defiance, a giving of the finger to Middle Age.

I used to think that 30 was middle-aged — of course I did not hold that opinion for long. And 40? I was just edging into my prime at 40. But fifty, the big five-oh? Face it. There's no denying that 50 is middle-aged. I have to wear a hat now because I'm bald, there's more white in my beard than brown, magazine ads selling prostate drugs earnestly inform me that the time has definitely come to bend over.

Middle Age . . . that great divide, over whose crest starts the irreversible downhill slalom, faster and faster . . . with no lift ticket back to the top.

Long ocean passages being something she more endures than enjoys, my wife's biggest birthday present to me on the Big Day was to be there at all. In addition, she baked a lovely cake with the last of our eggs and butter and gave me a bottle of good wine. My son gave me his best hat. We enjoyed perfect weather, the sky clear, the wind balmy but enough to move us along over gentle seas — a wonderful birthday. But the long awaited event was predictably anti-climactic; no enlightenment, no revelation beamed down from the sun by day nor from the moon by night. The vastness of the ocean puts a sharp pin to the balloon of human whimsy. I was still fifty.

A better understanding came piecemeal as the voyage unfolded. Ironically, it was my 18-year-old son who afforded me the best perspective. Children are the cardinal marks of a passage through life and the continuous interaction with my boy, as we worked the vessel across the Atlantic in fair weather and foul, helped me come to grips with what it meant to be 50.

Take the whale.

Just after dawn, weather extremely fine, we saw off the port bow a black ridge in the water—a blunt angular head exhaling a lacy mist — unmistakably a sperm whale. Imperturbable, it swam on a collision course with our bow.

We held our breaths as the great creature glided nearer. We kept our heading; assuming it would sense us and plunge, but on it came, steady as a planet. Just as I was about to alter course Diego, his eyes riveted on the whale, insisted,

"Keep going Dad — we can get a lot closer!"

Against my better judgment we kept on closing with the behemoth.

"OK, get ready to go about," I said.

"No, wait! Dad, it's so cool! Just a little closer! I've never seen one this close before. It's our chance!"

I hesitated another moment. Now we could see scars on its flank. A faint rainbow showed in its spume. It was at least fifty feet long, massive glistening, potent — and we were about to hit it!

I flung the wheel over. We missed it by a score of yards. Regal and serene, the whale kept going as though it never knew we were there. We all gazed at its slowly receding back in wonder — and then Diego reproached me for turning!

"It would have sensed us — whales aren't stupid, you know. We could have got so much closer!"

"What, you wanted to step off on its back? What if it didn't know we were there? You know, absent minded, lovelorn — and we suddenly smack it?"

"Unlikely...and we aren't going fast enough to hurt it anyway."

"Hurt the whale? What about us?"

"It couldn't hurt Breath's hull," he replied, confident, having watched me hand lay up 4 solid inches of fiberglass in the keel.

"Maybe, maybe not...but that fluke could mash up the rudder big time."

"We could fix it! Or else rig a steering oar from the staysail boom and balance the sails."

"Yeah... but why?"

"To look down its blow hole! Count its barnacles! Why not?"

Somehow this exchange left me feeling jaded...drearily pragmatic...old. Now I felt my fifty years. The 18-year-old, fiery and impetuous, was out for excitement and glory; I had been so too, at his age, but five decades had quite obviously weathered my stones. A hundred yards would have been close enough for me. Was I losing the spark? Fading?

Then there was the night of the gale. About 400 miles short of the Azores we heard on November Mike November's high seas forecast that a low was headed our way; then it got upgraded to a gale and was expected to be affecting us that night. The sky got heavily overcast, the wind increased to Force 6 and some nasty squalls persuaded us to reef the main and change to the small jib. Diego, Hotspur of the central north Atlantic, chafed at the slow progress in between squalls — his sights were set on Spain — but I liked the feeling that we were ready for the night.

At midnight a prolonged 40-knot blast had me crouching in the cockpit with one hand on the mainsheet and the other on the wheel, staring into howling blackness and pelting rain, shivering from the cold, wondering how much worse it might get. That's when we dropped the main altogether to jog along for the rest of the night on head sails and mizzen, warm and dry in our bunks, no alarms in the cold rainy dark — rather a good trade, I thought.

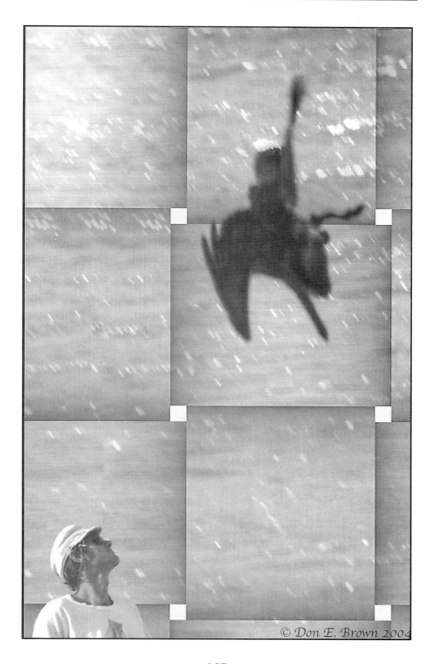

© Don E. Brown 2004

But Diego thought otherwise. "What's the matter dad? Breath can take it! Remember that 45-knot squall during the Thanksgiving regatta? We had everything flying, even the topsail! We even passed Fletcher!"

"Yes, our moment of glory — but that was a race, in protected waters — not a thousand miles from nowhere. Who are we trying to beat? The sea?"

"Ah, you're getting old and cautious, Pops."

"Damn right. I embrace it — it's also known as experienced and wise. No macho strivings on my boat — with a gale predicted! Me for a good night's sleep!"

Case closed — or so I thought. But after the bad squall the wind lessened drastically and the boat slogged along desultorily, making less than two knots. So where's this gale, Diego thought bitterly on his watch, as his life wasted away, minute by boring minute, until after an hour he could stand it no longer. He raised the main by himself and she finally started to move.

Then the wind began to rise again and she really started to move. Down below I felt the boat heel over til I was lying on the hull as much as on the bunk. Soon she was leaping along, crashing over waves, detonating bombs of froth that seethed past my ear.

Wind's back, I thought to myself. The boat's flying... but maybe Diego's right, got to drive her a little harder if we're ever going to get there... raised that heavy sail himself... good kid...

I drifted off into sleep — but woke as a gust like a punch from hell's hammer gun nailed the rail to the water. Simultaneously I felt drops of water on my face. Diego stood over me, dripping wet, and saying, "Dad Bad squall! We better get the main down fast!"

We leapt out the hatch, me in just my underwear, into a cold blast of rain. Charcoal clouds gorged with moisture hurtled close past the masthead. The only light came from angry phosphorescent welts whipped up off the sea's back. We staggered to the weather pin rail, and I cast off the halyards while Diego fought the sail down and Dorothy steered anxiously.

But something was wrong; the big mainsail wouldn't settle down into its lazyjacks; it kept exploding out of our grip, flogging itself like a demented Penitente with the 100-pound truncheon of our gaff. Someone could get maimed.

"Diego, the port lazy jack's parted! We've got to get a lashing around the whole thing!" I shouted. By searchlight we could see the lazyjack flying in the wind high out over the sea. I tried to throw a rope around the gaff but the billowing sail flung it back. The sea heaved the boat around so violently I needed both hands to hold on; the gaff was death to approach.

At that moment of impasse Diego sprang lightly into the mizzen shrouds, mounted the doghouse roof, deftly looped a rope around the gaff end, then took a wrap around the boom gallows. In short order he had quelled the uproar. It was daring and cool and happened before I could protest its danger.

We finally got lashings around the sail and I retired below, shaking uncontrollably with cold, a bit miffed at my orders having been ignored. Dorothy made two cups of steaming cocoa and handed them to me with a significant look — part warning, part plea — as I went back topside. I sat for a while with my son, resisting the impulse to upbraid him, and instead delivered a homily, the gist of which was:

"Diego, I am proud of your initiative and courage, but you need to learn more respect for the sea. Always remember, we're out here at the sea's sufferance — not as equals, certainly not as challengers. Because the sea can't lose. Only we can lose."

For once, my fiery young son listened meekly, then said,

"Dad, you were right about the main. Sorry."

Music to my ears. After clasping each other's shoulders, I went back to bed. It occurred to me there, descending into sleep, that a voyage is like a character drama acted on the empty stage of the sea, where nature writes the script, and the only audience is God.

As for the moral of the play...why, that varies from boat to boat, but as for me I felt comfortable with every hard won year of my half century by the time we got to Spain. I was glad to be 50 and glad to have an 18-year-old son. The boat needed both of us.

19.

SANTOS IN SEVILLA

By the time we got to Andalusia the weather became a matter of some concern. With the dangerous gales of the fall equinox approaching, and we in unfamiliar waters, it became time to find a spot to winter over.

This posed a problem.

We'd be spending half a year in close quarters, tied up to a dock, sandwiched between other boats. In the equanimable Caribbean we'd never lived that way for more than a few days at a time. It ran against the whole purpose of living afloat. Why pay to live in a floating trailer park when you could swing free to the wind in clean water, away from the constraints of land, especially immediate neighbors?

The crux of the problem was Santos. His barking could create difficulties in close quarters. I remembered my first encounter with a schipperke, at a dock in Nassau while delivering a boat to Miami. The dog barked piercingly every time someone set foot on the dock and there must have been twenty yachts berthed there, with people coming and going all the time. The little beast was maddening and its owners, two smug yuppies, did nothing to quell it. Childless, they doted on their dog — everybody else within earshot hated it.

It turned out that I had grounds for concern. Santos' hair-trigger bark did embroil us in acrimony more than once that winter. But, for the few who took offense, well...each of them were troubled characters, to say the least. And, for every enemy he made ten staunch friends. Everything considered, by spring-time when we finally left for the Aegean he had made his mark.

We had heard good things about Seville, that it was well protected, had a mild winter, a good marina, and was an inter-esting city. And it housed the famous Archives of the Indies, where I could pursue research on early West Indian history. We decided to give it a try.

Seville lies 55 miles up the Guadalquivir River. We entered the river mouth just after dawn, motoring over a sea of smoky yellow glass that reflected the ochre sunrise sky, following for miles the long stark line of blackened posts that marked the channel through the notoriously shifting sand bars.

Once we were within the compass of land the breeze lifted its head and began to blow — softly at first, fitful cat's paws over the water, then something steadier, widening ruffles with noticeable intent. We raised full sail and by the time the topsail was pulling 15 minutes later, Breath was heeled over on a beam reach, a stern wave riding her rudder, her wake burbling like early morning bird song. Soon she was bending to her work in earnest as the breeze became a wind and continued to freshen. The trees started to sway, the tall grass on the banks rippled with wind. We dropped the topsail and still the boat heeled enough to take water through her scuppers. Stronger gusts turned the river surface white...what was going on?

By midmorning the boat was reaming the narrowing river, the wind had reached gale force, we were deep-reefed and fly-ing, the stressed wake boiling up behind her as we passed lush meadows where noble steeds grazed and black bulls with upswept horns surveyed herds of plump cows. People on the bank stared, as we swept past. Eventually we dropped the main altogether and proceeded under headsails and mizzen, stag-gering along, caught by our first levanter, the violent easterly gale that can stop traffic in the Straits of Gibraltar.

Seville turned out to be a terrific place to spend the winter, but it wasn't without its drawbacks. It rained a hundred-year record that winter. The marina was a makeshift affair whose facilities were barely adequate — and grew worse as stragglers arrived. Worst of all, we had to play musical chairs with the electrical outlets — there were only 11 to supply 12 boats and we all depended on electrical heaters to keep warm.

We lay stern-to a floating dock by the riverbank. A shady tree overhung our stern and just ashore was a pleasant glade with benches around a fireplace. Across the street started a park, whose footpaths led past monuments, gardens and fountains to the edge of the city's old quarter where medieval battlements enclosed a labyrinth of narrow winding streets.

Around each corner of the old city lay another delight, perhaps a tiny plaza spilling over with flowers, or a cathedral with wonderfully carved stone doorways... an 11th century tower...tapas bars sunken with time three feet below the street level, where we ate enormous purple olives with wine drawn from casks that might have served Cervantes.

But Santos loved Seville for its park, where we happily took him for long and frequent walks. And truly, that was one marvelous park, a huge botanical garden planted with an unusually wide climactic range of trees and shrubs, enhanced by wrought iron benches and marble sculptures commemorating the worthy or the wealthy. Andalusian steeds in polished leather harness trotted by pulling wood coaches bright with varnish and gold leaf. In the middle of it lay a duck pond, and on the park's south border stood castles and palaces, built for the l929 world expo that never happened.

Seville represented the apex of Santos' watchdog career. Here he was the first line of defense not just for our boat but all the vessels wintering over at the floating dock. He had responsibilities; the threat was real.

Justly famous throughout Spain for its history, architecture, and flair, Seville was also infamous — for its thieves. All the way down the coast, when people heard we were headed for Seville they cautioned us against "chorizos," thieves, particularly purse snatchers mounted on motorbikes, operating in pairs, one driving and the other snatching. Chorizo translates literally as "sausage," which made no sense til I saw the police frisking a punk on a motor scooter. With his flashy clothes, pomaded hair and disrespectful smirk he was as slick as a salami.

Seville was also a traditional gypsy haven. Their plastic and cardboard encampments could suddenly appear against an old wall in an abandoned lot near the marina, here today gone tomorrow. Wandering over the bridge they could case the whole dock. We were cautious about buying in to the "gypsies are thieves" stereotype but common knowledge swore to it — and to see little gypsy children left with a showy sore and sad eyes to beg at the head of busy bridges made one less inclined to give their parents the benefit of the doubt.

The other boats had all been equally warned as they approached the fabled city. Already a bicycle had been stolen from the premises, a stainless steel, folding, made-for-boats — that is to say, expensive — model. So, when Santos arrived he filled a unanimously felt need for a good watchdog. And since there were no other dogs aboard he also filled the role of marina mascot. Inevitably he attracted controversy.

He kept strict watch, enough to please even the most paranoid property owner. And he barked... for many reasons, some for hard causes such as a cat, a rat or someone, anyone, entering the dock area. He also barked on general principle; it was the time-hallowed duty of his breed to voice warnings. Our security was his responsibility, and like an Israeli general he was determined to err on the side of caution. He would take no chances. He would not be hushed. And he made it clear that he obeyed a higher law than just his master's say-so.

Most of our neighbors appreciated his contribution. The first to react was Marika, the Dutch girlfriend of a young Italian doctor on a fifty-foot pilothouse ketch. She was a bouncy good-looking blonde, who had wrinkled up her pretty nose when she heard we were Americans.

"Americans..." she said with an obvious lack of enthusiasm. "I hope you won't anchor too close to us." But when she saw Santos her face lit up. She was starved for a pet, loved dogs, and fell for Santos' affable fox face. She soon became a friend and warned us that the gratuitous racism and fatuous bragging of the two Americans already there had stereotyped our nation as being populated by right-wing, loudmouthed boors, smug about money. I came as a signal exception on all three counts, being left-wing, self-conscious and more or less broke.

Anyway, Santos became the mascot of the dock, the recipient of carefully wrapped bags of bones, gristle and skin that otherwise would have gone to the garbage. It helped that being a small dog and a fastidious one he could eat chicken bones without danger of choking. At the Sunday potlucks he was beckoned from bench to bench to do his tricks for scraps.

However, three of our dock mates made it abundantly clear that he was not welcome around them. They were two besotted Englishmen and an old John Bircher with a lecherous smirk who had sailed from California, and what a piece of work each was! We got to know them all too well.

The trouble of course was his bark — not when we were around because we rode tight herd on him, physically restraining him or taking him down below where he never barked. But three days a week, Dorothy was off to work in the Spanish shipyard at 6:45, then Diego went to school, and I went to the Archives to read 16th century governors' letters from the east Caribbean. From 8 til 3 nobody was home except the doggus, and he was bored, and pent up.

Unfortunately, a redheaded Briton with a temper lived on the boat next door. He wasn't a bad sort, but he was irascible and opinionated. Typical of a certain segment of frustrated English sailors squeezed for cash he harbored a residual prejudice against American yachtsmen, whom it comforted him to characterize as rich dilettantes with expensive cocktail yachts. In our case he was put out by the fact that we actually had the most traditional boat at the dock, had put in the most sea miles — and had built it ourselves.

"Firebeard" stayed up late of nights drinking rotgut red wine packaged in a paper box — it was cheap, he was poor. Not surprisingly, he slept late many mornings nursing his head. Invariably, then it was that a stray dog, some loitering, malingering ill-bred cur, would wander casually onto the bridge and insolently peer down and give Santos the canine equivalent of the finger. Never one to bear slights meekly, he would bristle like a porcupine and peal out an all points alarm, thereby jabbing a hot poker into the Brit's sensitized brain.

It didn't take Firebeard long to confront me. "That sod of a dog! Not even a proper dog, a...a bloody rodent! A felonious nuisance! He barks all day long at people on the dock! at rats on the bank! at people walking on the bridge! He even barks at the bleeding aeroplanes!"

He had a valid point, but fortunately we were able to ignore it because the next boat down, a big steel ketch, held a very different view. Pierre and Toni were affable Dutch burghers, Toni plump and cute with shy but dancing eyes, Pierre lean and sinewy with a tall brush cut of gray hair. He had been a pilot in a big Dutch port and spoke any number of languages including fluent English. As opinionated as Firebeard, he liked Santos just the way he was — especially his barking.

"Don't hush the dog — he's a fine watchdog, he protects the whole dock. Let him bark so much he can! Good boy!" He'd say, and reward him with something saved from supper.

Pierre was quite concerned about thievery — it had been his bicycle stolen and his beamy 48-foot boat was loaded with expensive electronics, a new outboard, brand new gear. He blamed the bike's loss on gypsies. He'd bought another bike, even more expensive, and had chained it to a tree on the bank and was always chasing off boys who wandered near the dock without good reason, especially if they were swarthy.

No love was lost between Pierre and Firebeard. Pierre thought the Englishman a cantankerous runt and Firebeard thought Pierre to be a moral weakling because he lived in such a comfortable boat. He despised people in boats bigger than his own 25-foot no-standing-headroom cutter. The only way to go to sea that showed competence and mettle was in small boats — small wooden boats, in fact. Steel or fiberglass were for the unskilled and the cowardly. When Pierre heard that he burst out laughing.

Santos added fuel to the fire between them. That became apparent one afternoon when I came back early to the boat. I heard Santos raise the alarm to a suspicious rustling on the bank, then heard Firebeard bellow a curse, "Shut the [expletive deleted] up, you sod!" — hard followed by Pierre's exuberant shout, "Good dog! Bark, Santos, bark!"

Around November the word came down from the port authority that the new bridge under construction just a couple hundred yards down the river was going to be welded shut. It was to be a drawbridge but wouldn't be open til early spring. The boaters were officially warned; anyone who didn't leave now would effectively be locked in for the winter — unless they wanted to pull their masts out.

Firebeard fretted and fumed — and finally left. One afternoon his boat was gone. His job, renovating a house, had ended. We heard he went to Cadiz where he had friends and work. Almost a year later we heard his boat had been lost at sea en route back to England.

A few spaces down the dock lived another of Santos' detractors, Thomas, a friend of Firebeard's. He too was British, a wooden boat purist and he also had problems with alcohol — in fact, poor Thomas was a suicidal alcoholic. We visited him on his boat once and watched him methodically smoke two pipes of hashish while downing tumblerful after tumblerful of the raw box wine guaranteed to produce a splitting headache.

He was thin and pallid with wispy strands of sandy hair combed over the top of his head. His weak eyes blinking through horn-rimmed glasses made him look a bit like an owl — and like one he shunned daylight. He'd go out at night to get a different venue for his drinking, and come staggering back in the wee hours, his great coat hugged tight, a deathly pallor on his face, his eyes concentric whorls of dizziness. He'd collapse in his cockpit and, eventually, retch over the side. At 3 a.m. the river was silent as a sepulcher; and as water carries sound, the agonized spasms of Thomas's body getting rid of self-inflicted poison must have reached all the way to the second bridge.

Thomas had some source of income — his upper crust accent

suggested he was a "remittance man" paid by a respectable family to be disreputable somewhere far from home. Since he needed more money, he hoped to sell his boat, a handsome, well-built 40-foot wood yawl that had once been owned by a famous yachtsman — but even from a distance one saw signs of egregious neglect. The varnish had peeled off the mast, dirt and mold back-filled the corners of the deck; every scupper hole had its streak running down the hull. Down below was gloomy, dark wood and dirty velvet, roaches crawling over unwashed dishes, and empty wine cartons. An unsettling odor clung to the interior, perhaps sewage leaked from the head, or swamp gas emitted by the bilge, or a dribble of overlooked spew... whatever, I couldn't wait to get back topsides for a deep draught of clean winter air.

Like Firebeard, Thomas extolled wood boats over fiberglass — "plastic" boats were just so many clorox bottles littering the sea — and also liked to complain that there were "no real seamen" left these days. He would look around the dock, disdain on his face as he pined for the company of true grit skippers. Us Americans were inherently undeserving of consideration, even though each of us had crossed an ocean to get there. And the French! Nothing they did was of any merit.

Yet when one begged for a detail of his own sea experience he had to admit that he hadn't even brought his boat across the English Channel — a friend had skippered the boat across. Now there was a real stalwart! And he would wax euphoric about the gales that worthy had weathered, the vessels delivered, the emergencies surmounted. "There is the real thing!" he'd say grandly. "This lot!...Pretenders!" he muttered scornfully, offended by the mediocrity which surrounded him.

And he sided with Firebeard about the dog. At the potluck as Santos made his rounds checking for scraps Thomas would shy away from the little dog as though it were a sewer rat. "Nasty little beast! Infernal nuisance!" His Irish girlfriend, Molly, always looked a little torn. She clearly liked animals and had a nurturing nature, which must have been the reason she stayed with Thomas, he needed help so much.

At any rate the dog did not lack for scraps or cuddling at

the convivial potlucks. He was generally recognized to be an asset to the little community. Not only was he a top-notch watch dog, he was also — perhaps more importantly — a world-class pre-emptive ratter. Before we arrived rats had vandalized a couple of the yachts in their nasty, profligate way; with a trumpet flourish of satisfaction Pierre had proclaimed that a schipperke's chief duty on the medieval grain barges was To Guard Against Rats. Being Dutch he was presumed to know.

Rats are a scourge afloat — smart, disgusting, incredibly destructive, and with a million hiding places. One rat can ruin a whole bin of vegetables in a night, never sating itself with one carrot or peach, but sampling widely and defecating freely. During the day, hunkered down in the far recesses of the boat, they gnaw on electric insulation and engine hose, causing unforeseeable failures.

While others installed elaborate rat guards we relied on Santos. He fully understood that rats were unquestioned hereditary enemies who needed constant surveillance and intimidation — the which he eagerly provided. Alert, restless, avid for distinction, he convinced them that, at all costs, they must not be found in his domain.

To this end Santos spent hours every day worrying an old coconut husk that had stayed with us across the Atlantic. Its stiff hair-like fibers made a perfect rat effigy and Santos ostentatiously savaged it, gnawing, growling, whining, holding it between his forepaws, tearing at it with his jaws low to the deck, his rump high, poised to leap.

He especially loved to shake it back and forth in a blur — trying to break its neck — then toss it up and leap upon it with a bloodcurdling snarl and a snap, catching it before it came to rest. He would work it all the way down the deck and back, in frenzy, totally absorbed in dismembering this infinitely hated other.

Any rats on the bank could not fail to see their death being practiced by this slavering killer whose great hope in life was to get his jaws on a live rat. They watched bleakly from their rat holes, their beady eyes weighing opportunity versus risk, while he dared them to make his day.

© Don E. Brown 2004

At any rate we never got a rat aboard and neither did our neighbors. Santos' aggressive patrolling must have sent them elsewhere. Pierre made much of this at the Sunday potlucks, calling him over for pats and holding out a bit of gristle from his plate, getting the little dog worked up, til he was prancing and jumping eagerly — then he would toss it away shouting "Rat, Santos! Rat!" Santos would shoot off like a bolt from a crossbow, his acceleration a wonder to behold.

Santos was a great prop for Dorothy's English lessons. These started with Jaime and Carmen, the children of the marina owners, but soon expanded through word of mouth and would have become a full-time occupation had we stayed any longer. The dog acted as greeter when students arrived at the boat and entertained them if they had to wait for another lesson to finish. One of Santos' favorites was Isabela, a medical student, who always arrived a little early to give Santos a treat.

Then there was the patrician lady of Dorothy's own age who lived in an elegant apartment and received her and Santos for lessons with tea and pastries. She spoke no English at all , but she greatly enjoyed the lessons, the two women switching languages in mid-sentence as they attempted to communicate, laughing until they choked. Dorothy and her unusual dog were a breath of sea air and spice from exotic lands in that immaculate, richly furnished, tastefully decorated penthouse. Her husband was head of the famous Seville shipyard and he spoke good English. When he inquired as to his wife's progress one day when he came home early from work Dorothy somewhat worriedly confided that, well...actually... The husband put up his hand to stop her from saying any more. With a broad smile he declared, "Very good— she loves the lessons!"

Andy was the last of the triumvirate who took offense at Santos' presence in the marina. We met at our first Sunday potluck, where the marina residents gathered around a fire for food and drink and conversation. The air got a little nippy and the fire was a warm cheerful crackle. I joined a small group — a British couple and Andy. We introduced ourselves; the Brits seemed decent and sincere but I didn't like the look of my compatriot. He was about 60, with white hair in a long crew cut, and a somewhat weasely cast to his pinched features. He resumed telling how he'd gotten to Seville.

"I worked hard all my life...had two businesses, used to get up at 5 a.m. and work til dark. When I'd made my money I decided I wanted to see the world from the deck of my own boat. I bought my vessel, prepared it for years, but my wife didn't like sailing — seasick — didn't want to leave her home and the kids. We'd been thirty years there in southern California. So I dumped her. I needed my freedom. There were oceans to sail, good lookin' women to..." he wiggled his eyebrows lewdly. "My wife cried, said she'd try it, keep our marriage together...but I figured she'd just bitch and moan and spoil my fun. So I divorced her, gave her the house, and off I sailed."

Uncomfortable silence. His self depiction was so raw, so personal. Without knowing anything about his wife I found myself feeling he should have given her a try — after thirty years! But maybe she was happier without him.

Andy and I were polite, but we avoided each other — until Santos sparked a confrontation.

Having come late to Seville we were tied up to the end of the dock closest to the bridge — not a good berth. Noise and dust from passing vehicles drifted down and occasionally a bad boy might throw an orange onto our deck and run away laughing. But by far the worst of it was the nearby traffic light that made a sound so invasive we could scarcely bear it. It was harsh, metallic, jarring, like the sound of a cash register mixed with a car grinding its gears. Loud on calm nights it was even audible in rain and wind, going "whirr...chuk! ...whirr... chuk!" day and night without cease.

So when the chance came to move to a better space we only hesitated because it was exactly between Andy and Thomas. And sure enough, at the Sunday potluck when I mentioned our intention of moving, Andy strode over to confront me.

"You bring that goddamn black beast next to my boat it's war between us, buster. You'll be sorry."

Everyone fell silent at this unseemly breach of good feeling.

Andy stalked off to his boat.

Thomas kept his peace til most people had gone back to their conversations, then he came up, reasonably sober, and said with the utmost intensity, shaking slightly "You can't be serious about moving alongside with that horrid little dog.... it would be unconscionable... criminal!" Molly, his girlfriend, wouldn't meet my eyes.

Andy's bluntness tempted me to defy him, but Thomas's relatively polite Oxbridge plea made me admit that if one didn't like dogs then having a Santos close by could be unpleasant. So we gave up the idea. The thing is, none of the other boats would have objected to our moving alongside. They accepted Santos as a useful and amusing member of the community and were willing to make allowances. Then again, they weren't next door to him.

Things came to a head in the early spring. We finally found out why the facilities at the dock were so poor. All winter we had shared one spigot for fresh water, and it often dry. There was only one shower, housed in a drafty cinderblock shack, never finished and on the verge of collapse, whose cement floor was lethally slippery with moss, whose cracked light switch gave off sharp tingles of electricity. To get hot water you had to put a match to an ancient rusted gas blower, which ignited with a roar and an upward whoosh of flame that boded no good.

When we complained we always got a profuse apology and a runaround from Jorge and Maria— now it became clear why. The marina lived on borrowed time. It had been set up at a disused city dock, but the authorities now wanted the space back for the upcoming World Expo. Jorge wasn't giving up without a fight, and he had some legal claim involving an escrow account that they wanted to give back to him but he refused to accept.

Impasse. So to pressure him the port authority decided to pressure us, his customers, by making difficulties about the supply of water and electricity — they cut us off. Where we had been sharing outlets and making do, now there was no electricity at all. Presumably their idea was to get the marina tenants to move out, but, the bridge being welded shut for the foreseeable future and the only other marina located a half hour's drive out of town, there was really no place else to go.

Hence we were receptive to Jorge's proposal — that we mount a demonstration at the port authority headquarters nearby. He and Maria arrived at the Sunday potluck with cloth banners that we painted with symbols and slogans while Jorge cooked a special paella in a huge wok, copiously garnished with chicken, mussels and shrimp tucked into the steaming saffron rice bubbling over the open fire. We feasted, drank wine and made our plans for the morning.

Bright and early we marched down to the three story Port Authority headquarters to greet the executives as they arrived. We set up the banners — "Queremos agua y luz!" (We want water and light!) Blanca, a fiery young Peruvian mother was a veteran of street protests in Lima and Santiago. She had her infant strapped to her front, a baby bottle in one hand and an empty water bucket in the other. As the first official arrived he had to ease his car slowly over a dip into the driveway. We raised a loud chant — "We want power and light!" and Blanca rushed over to his car window brandishing her baby and wailed, "My baby! My baby needs water!" Then she grabbed the metal bucket and beat it mercilessly with a steel ladle, setting up one hellacious din. I recoiled in middle class propriety but there was no stopping Blanca. The bureaucrat hurried into the refuge of his building, not glancing to one side or the other.

The other execs did the same and soon we could see them huddled together and looking out their windows. We kept up our shouts, Blanca making a god-awful racket at erratic intervals. A crowd gathered on the street. Within fifteen minutes we were asked to send in negotiators. Carlos (Blanca's husband) and I got chosen to meet with the boss, a middle-aged man with a sagging belly and worry lines on a decent face. We put it to him that, whatever the rights of the case, it was wrong to penalize us, who had come here for winter shelter, in all good faith.

I noticed that every time Blanca bastinadoed her bucket he squeezed his eyes shut in pain. He was scarcely listening to us, and inside of ten minutes he agreed to provide better water and power if we would just stop that woman! He proved good to his word — the next morning workmen arrived to put in a bank of proper spigots and outlets.

While we were demonstrating, the only person left at the dock was Thomas. He had staggered back late the night before, and about now he woke up with the usual splitting headache and disabling nausea — to a peal of Santos' barking. It was loud and frantic, even by his standards, and it didn't subside — it increased.

"Molly, for the love of God throw a bloody knife at that bloody yapping freak!"

No answer.

He burrowed his head under his pillow. Each yip bull-whipped his cerebellum. No one was making even the slightest effort to hush the dog up. Then he remembered. Everyone was at the demonstration. The dock was deserted. Santos went on, gale force paroxysms of barks, accelerating to a storm.

Intoxicated with fury, Thomas finally bolted out of bed, grabbed a machete and stormed on deck, almost naked, pallid as a grub, grimacing with pain and hatred, screaming curses — and brandishing a weapon. Two youths who were crouched at the base of a tree next to the dock looked up in consternation, dropped something, vaulted the old iron fence and disappeared into the bridge traffic.

Thomas stopped dead in his tracks. Pierre's expensive bicycle was chained to the base of that tree. A hacksaw blade, one end wrapped with tape, lay in the grass. The chain was cut halfway through. Adrenaline steam-cleaned Thomas's brain when he realized that he'd single handedly run off two thieves.

He next realized that Santos had gone quiet. The little dog was poised at the stern of our boat, looking eagerly towards Thomas, his stub of a tail jerking back and forth, only an occasional yelp shuddering out to vent his feelings.

The incident changed Thomas's feelings about the dog — and about life. When we returned everyone wanted to hear the story. Thomas was quite decent, giving the dog full credit, deprecating his own part. Pierre responded handsomely, thanking Thomas profusely and giving him a very good bottle of wine. Thomas, naturally, enjoyed the attention — and started to mellow out about the dog.

"For once that perpetual noise machine had good reason to bark...once, after six months of din!" But he said it with a noticeable lack of rancor.

At the next potluck he continued to harrumph about "that noise machine," but added in a conciliatory tone: "A nuisance but apparently a necessary one, and certainly the lesser of two evils, by Jove." Molly felt emboldened to pat Santos surreptitiously and by the end of the evening he lay on his back in her lap while she scratched his belly. The next week I noticed Santos wolfing down beans and ham hock from a plate next to Thomas's feet, while Thomas talked to a neighbor.

"Santos! What do you think you're doing? Come here! Thomas, I'm so sorry — he never usually does that!"

Thomas looked a bit sheepish.

"It's all right. I...uh...gave it to him.. Put the miserable beast to some use cleaning up... saves doing the dishes . . ."

From this time on a cloud lifted from Thomas's brow. The early morning vomiting stopped. He and Molly attended the potlucks more frequently and when we left for the Aegean he seemed genuinely sorry to see the dog go.

Santos made his mark in Seville.

20.

PASSAGE TO PALERMO

The quavering call of the muezzin reached us faintly through the calm afternoon air, drifting out from behind the stone parapets of an ancient Carthaginian port. Zephyrs barely filled our topsail as we ghosted away from the tanned African hills and eased into the lambent blue of the Skerki Passage. We were bound for Sicily.

Midnight found us on a dark sea gazing at brilliant stars, constellations that brought to mind the myths of antiquity. The peace of the night made a bittersweet backdrop to the turbulence that had rocked these shores in ancient times. Here, high in a cave above Sicily's western shores, Odysseus had plunged a sharpened stake into the Cyclops' eye. Here pirates had pillaged since the dawn of navigation. And here a sudden Sicilian tempest once sank a huge Roman fleet and drowned a hundred thousand men all at once.

So many ghosts on the empty sea. In the dreamy reaches of my long night watch I found myself wondering if so many simultaneously expiring souls would leave some kind of disturbance, a standing wave in the ether, a psychic black hole... A fanciful thought — but one that was to crop up again and again by the time we finally reached Palermo. What else would explain the eventfulness of the brief passage from Africa to Europe?

A light popped up on the horizon, then another and another, til fifteen or twenty boats showed in a tight cluster ahead. Fishing boats? If so, they were oddly grouped. We altered course enough to give them a wide berth.

Suddenly another vessel switched on its lights nearby and steamed toward us on what appeared to be a collision course. Being under sail we had the right of way so we kept our heading, but being prudent we turned on the strobe light at the top of our mast. The ship kept coming. We aimed a spotlight at its bridge, to no avail. Was anybody on the bridge? There was still time enough for us to pass ahead so we started the engine and crossed clear of his bow, watching his running lights anxiously. But just as we breathed a sigh of relief, the ship turned — towards us! — and poured on the steam.

I redlined our big Ford with a burst of smoke and a hammering of pistons that sucked down the stern, thrust us forward, and dragged a steep wave in tow. Again the ship turned towards us. He could see us all right; he had us in his sights!

By now he was so close we could see his bow wave sparkling with phosphorescence. I flung over the wheel and conceded rights of tonnage, waiting furiously for him to pass; but to our amazement he stopped, turned, and headed slowly back to the north. We sailed south for half an hour to put distance between us, and then tried our course again. The ship aimed for us and put on speed and at the last minute we turned back and stopped. It turned back and stopped. We watched each other.

So we gave it up and spent the rest of the night going the long way around the fishing fleet — if that's what it was. By now I was sure something nasty was going on. With the Mafia to the east, Col. Gaddaffi to the south and PLO headquarters to the west, anything could be happening — guns, heroin, terrorism...?

The fleet dispersed rapidly an hour before dawn and we were motoring eastwards when, silhouetted against the vermilion and gold promise of a sunrise was the distinctive profile of the ship that had run us off, dead in the water. We kept going and passed a couple hundred yards from a grey naval vessel with gun turrets fore and aft, but with no flag, no markings, nor any sign of life aboard. After ten minutes it steamed off towards the southwest. It must have wanted to inspect us in daylight. We wondered why. Some of the possibilities gave me a chill.

What with the 6-hour delay and the dying wind we gave up making port that day and resigned ourselves to the sea's timetable. Gradually a breeze filled in from the southwest bringing with it a haze that reduced visibility to less than five miles. Late in the day we were looking for Capo San Vito, the high promontory at the NW extremity of Sicily. GPS was still in the future.

A bold cliff appeared, as if by magic, out of the haze at last. It soared up from the sea, a fractured crag that had been battered by the elements since creation. Nothing grew on its seamed face; but a 12th-century fortress, built out of the mountain rock, stood on a narrow cliffside ledge where its stones must have been quarried. There was no beach below it, no port to lord it over, no straits to dominate — just the wide sea beyond. Why had it been built? A lookout, a last redoubt? Standing alone in the haze, it had the force of a vision.

But was this Capo San Vito? The contours we saw didn't quite fit the chart's description. The land dropped away too fast, instead of curving slowly to the southeast. My wife thought it must be Isole Marettimo, some twenty miles short of Capo San Vito; but I refused to believe we'd made such slow progress and blamed the haze for the discrepancies with the chart. The dramatic promontory with its mythic castle looked too magnificent, surely the rampart of a major landmass, not some insignificant islet.

But, as often proved the case when Dorothy ventured a navigational opinion, she was right — my wife has the instincts of a migrating bird. So we accommodated ourselves to yet another delay and finally picked up the Capo San Vito light by midnight. The sky had cleared enough to see a few stars and we were about ten miles off when we saw more lights, spread out in no discernible pattern everywhere across our course. They had to be tunny nets. We'd be all night going around them.

The pilot book had a long paragraph about tunny nets. They stretch for many miles out from the coast, and are owned by whole villages. A fleet of boats sets them, each vessel carrying out a segment to hook together at sea. They are poorly lit, very expensive, and are guarded by fishermen who grow easily enraged. I had a dread of fouling one of these nets because the only other time we had sailed in Sicilian waters we had hooked one. That incident was tatooed into my psyche.

On that occasion Dorothy and I were with my parents, retired missionaries, in their 32-foot ketch. We had spent an exhilarating day surging at hull speed down the spectacular north coast, but after a beautiful sunset darkness found us five miles offshore motoring east in flat calm. The stars reflected all around us in the smooth seas as my mother, to great acclaim, produced a deep dish of sumptuous lasagna hot from the oven. The only traffic visible appeared to be a coastal freighter some five miles ahead of us, its stern light dim on the horizon. We opened an excellent bottle of Spanish Rioja and toasted the delights of the cruising life.

"At this moment there is absolutely nowhere I'd rather be," said I.

"Here's to the glorious coast of Sicily!" declaimed my father, cup held high.

"Good God! What's that?" exclaimed my mother in alarm, pointing.

The stern light of the vessel that only moments ago had been five miles ahead was now bobbing past, scarcely ten feet distant. It wasn't a stern light; it was a kerosene lantern riding the sea on a cork life ring — and it triggered a memory. I had seen such lights in Palermo on a fishing boat, and had thought it a quaint way to mark a net. This train of thought came to an obvious and alarming conclusion in synchronicity with our boat, which came very gradually to a halt although the motor chugged on unfazed.

"Cut the engine!" I shouted and as it stopped we felt ourselves moving unmistakably backwards.

"I think we've caught a net." We looked over the side with

a flashlight and saw a ¾-inch line passing tightly under the boat. I tried to dislodge it with an oar but couldn't get it free. It suddenly grew very quiet out there on the glossy sea. The lights of land gave an oblivious, peaceful glow.

"What are we going to do?" asked Dorothy, as I poked unavailingly at the line.

"We may have to cut it," I said, uncomfortably, recalling the pilot book's warning.

Just then my mother observed that there was a searchlight in the distance that seemed to be pointed our way — and sure enough, we soon could see a fishing boat at full throttle, its foredeck crowded with men shouting and waving their fists. Ever practical, Mom dove below to look up apologies in an English-Italian phrase book. My dad and I worked feverishly with the oar and a boat hook, but the damn net was stuck fast. We could push it away but it sprang right back.

The fishermen pulled up close, fixed us point blank in the glare of their spotlight, and poured out abuse. We didn't need a command of Italian to understand that we were pathetic dilettantes! — a threat not only to ourselves, a trifling matter, but also to hardworking fishermen whose precious net we were mutilating! Which was a very serious matter, by the look of it a capital offense. We were exquisitely conscious that this was Sicily — we'd all seen The Godfather. How would they deal with us — strangle us with piano wire? Behead the ship's cat? It was incumbent on us to do something decisive, dramatic...and fast.

I called for a mask and snorkel, and then very deliberately took off my shirt. The uproar subsided noticeably. Then I dropped my trousers and stood buck naked in the spotlight. That cut off the hubbub like a guillotine. Obviously, I took this matter very seriously. I respected their net.

Emboldened by the dead hush, I slipped into the water and motioned for the searchlight. They jumped to redirect it. I took a deep breath and dived, careful not to gaze into the panicky black abyss, and followed the rope under the hull to where a strand of net was caught on a protruding bolt at the base of the starboard bilge keel. I plucked it off, then shot to the surface and vaulted out of the water in one seamless motion, as though a shark were at my heels.

The boat drifted free. My mother said loudly, "What a man!" Clearly the Sicilians agreed. Not only were they old-fashioned enough to be shocked by nudity — or perhaps it was the scandalous lack of underwear — but few of them know how to swim and in any event would never dream of entering the water at night. They were powerfully mollified, and with an old world courtesy that bordered on the deferential they indicated the way around the rest of their nets. We resumed the voyage with our new friends bidding us heartfelt farewells til we were out of earshot.

This incident returned to mind like an acid flashback as I surveyed the hopeless hodge-podge of lights off Capo San Vito. Determined to make no more night swims, especially since I now knew that sharks were attracted by fish struggling in the nets, we stopped the boat and rocked in gentle seas while I climbed the ratlines to get a higher perspective. I returned to the deck without a clue, wondering if we'd have to heave to all night or just plow through and hope for the best, when suddenly we heard the approaching roar of an engine. The sound grew closer but we saw no running lights. Then a blacked-out, very fast boat loomed out of the night, pulled alongside and stopped.

This was no fishing trawler — it looked like a big Hatteras or Bertram, expensive and powerful. Someone shouted a question in Italian. I asked one back in English — which way around the nets? They conferred for a minute then waved at me to follow, so we did, running our engine top speed to keep their stern light in view. We ran for almost half an hour north, hoping they knew where they were going. I wasn't at all convinced they had comprehended my question about the nets.

Suddenly they cut off their stern light, and disappeared in a blizzard of foam. What had happened to our guide? Lights still dotted the distance everywhere we looked.

Moments later, out of the south came another drone, which increased into a roar — and then a searchlight pinned our rig. Up sizzled an enormous racing machine with an evil stilletto bow. It dropped off its plane with a bow-heavy lurch, its engines growling and coughing in idle like a brace of angry leopards. The spotlight blinded; a rattle of hostile Italian smote us about the ears. A hardfaced, burly man of about 40 was leaning over the foredeck rail waiting impatiently for an answer.

Now what...?

I shouted back, "Sorry, can you speak English?" There was a startled silence and then another fellow climbed onto the foredeck.

"Where you are headed?"

"Palermo."

"Why you steering north if you go for Palermo?" he asked suspiciously.

"Because these damned tunny nets are everywhere," I said. "How do you get past them?"

"What is you nationality?"

"American...but listen, can you guide me through the nets?"

"Have you seen some boat here this night?"

"Yes, a big sports fisherman ...he left five minutes ago."

"Which way? Which way he go?"

"That way, north."

He whirled away and snapped an order at the bridge. The engines bellowed, the boat catapulted forward, and I got a glimpse of uniforms and automatic weapons in the cockpit.

"Wait — what about the nets?" I yelled.

"To hell with nets — go straight to Palermo!"

They left us in a backwash of froth, breathing exhaust fumes.

Breath finally reached Palermo as the city's last lights undulated and bounced on the swell. The early morning air was scented with maquis, and mist clung like damp fleece to the upland valleys. We watched the sun slowly pull itself free of the horizon. Then, from top to bottom it broke into dazzling flame, repelling sight, suffusing the sea with fiery orange light. We entered the breakwater, leaving behind our wake spreading over the glassy sea, each wavelet like a slowly subsiding life.

21.

THE TINKER OF CORFU TOWN

Perhaps Corfu was an obvious place for ghosts to come swirling out of the past. Enough unsettled business has happened there in the last 5000 years to saturate the ether with apparitions so thick that a slight jog, any disturbance, may precipitate, out of solution as it were, some pathetic shade that hovers about dolefully beating its wings and fanning forth the grievance of its times.

We left Brindisi in the afternoon bound for Corfu, picked up a freshening breeze, and ran down the heel of Italy, past an empty coastline of layered cliffs with occasional towns situated high atop, overlooking the sea. The absence of seaside villages underscored a brutal history of piracy that plagued this coast for millennia. Towns built on the water got sacked. Towns built on the heights could see ships approaching in time to flee or to prepare their defenses.

Piracy was a respectable occupation in the days of Odysseus who pillaged innocent seaside settlements when opportunity offered; and later when the Roman Empire declined, a long era of pillage began anew, reaching its apex when much of the Greek, Italian and Spanish coasts were depopulated by slave raiders from North Africa.

To sail down these shores and see the whitewashed towns still perched on their cliffs gave flesh to that history.

All night the breeze held up and in the morning it freshened, driving us along the building seas towards the snow-capped peaks of Albania, brilliant in the clear sunlit air. Close to our south the solid green mass of Corfu rose out of Homer's wine-dark Ionian Sea. By the time we reached the Albanian line and jibed, the wind had increased to near gale force and we thundered down the long scenic channel between Corfu and the mainland. Wild flowers decked the summer hillsides as long gusts fell off the slopes and laid Breath rail down and drove her hard through the flat water of the channel.

Next day we explored the town, Santos prancing and pulling at his leash, afire with eagerness to be ashore on an island so ancient with odors. After taking in the impressive town square with its stately stone buildings, broad promenades and wide avenues, we wandered away into a less pretentious part of town and a much older one.

We ended up in the bazaar, a maze of narrow alleyways still paved by cobblestones and lined cheek to jowl by tiny hole-in-the-wall shops whose tent-tattered awnings stretched out over the street and blocked out the sky, a warren isolated in time and place, selling a curious variety of goods — linens, shoes, postcards, tools, jewelry, sandals, pots and pans, umbrellas, carvings, paintings, tin and brassware. From the look and sound of it many of the items for sale were being made on the premises. Dorothy and I went with the flow of people, enjoying the crowd, looking into the small shops while Santos walked close beside us. He was never enthused about walking in a crowd where he couldn't see and was liable to be stepped on.

A throng of people like a torpid river at full slack tide eddied into every nook and cranny. Greeks and Italians and legions of tourists, especially British and German, but especially German. If the phrase "ugly American" was coined for and ever deserved by the Yankee tourist for being fat, affluent, heedless of local sensibilities, expensive camera and above all loud — in the Mediterranean that mantle has passed on to the German. Now the deutsche mark reigns supreme and breeds an irksome self-satisfaction. Loud Teutonic voices were an inescapable backdrop to the hubbub of artisanry.

As we slowly jostled our way down the narrow winding streets we came to the stall of a tinsmith. An old white-haired man sat at a worn workshop table hammering with a small ball-peen hammer at a funnel. He was bent over his work, oblivious of the crowd, and his wares hung in clusters about the front of his shop — teapots, funnels of all sizes, cups, bowls, plates, flower vases. Taptaptap went the hammer, as he turned the sheet of tin against a mold. This was hand craftsmanship little changed in centuries. I wondered who this tinker was, whether he'd learned the trade from his father, whether his family occupation reached far back to tinkers' guilds, medieval fairs and farmyards.

He reached his arm out for a different hammer and my idyll on the harmony of history shriveled. His forearm bore a grisly tattoo, the infamous thunderbolt and prisoner ID number. I'd seen it before on ravaged old men riding the New York subway, clinging to an overhead strap — it always sent a chill of horror through me, like a recurring nightmare when the face of a stranger sitting next to me at a bar, turns and smiles and morphs into the face of the devil, full of unimaginable evil — smiling at me.

This old tinsmith had survived Hitler's death camps. Loutish German voices haggling in the street suddenly seemed insupportable.

I decided to buy a funnel — a boat always needs another funnel.

When I spoke to him, in English, he looked up eagerly, as I thought for a sale. But no, his first words were a question.

"English? You English people?"

"No," I said. "We're American."

"American!" he exclaimed with outright joy. "Oh Americans... the best people! American soldiers save me. I love American!" He jumped up and almost embraced me and urged me out of the street into his shop. Just then Dorothy appeared at the shop front, with Santos on the leash still hidden behind the counter.

"My wife..." I said.

He gave her a look that resonated with feeling, so intense it startled her. But he mastered himself and urged her kindly, "Come in, please, come..."

"Thank you, but I have a dog...this little dog...is it alright?" she asked cautiously. Santos appeared in the doorway, a ray of light from a gap in the awning illuminating him. The old man gasped.

"Pauli!" he exclaimed. "Pauli..." followed by endearments in what sounded like Italian. He dropped to his knees and held out his arms. Santos, usually aloof with strangers, was happy to escape the trodding crowd of feet outside and he trotted amiably over and nuzzled his arm as the old guy ran his fingers through his ruff and scratched behind his ears like he'd done it a thousand times. When at last he got up his eyes were glistening and he told us, almost dreamily, "Before the war I have dog, like this...just like this."

We asked about his war experience and it came pouring out. He had been an Italian Jew caught up in the clutches of the "final solution." He spent a year in Auschwitz and in the last month it was touch and go whether they would be exterminated before the Allies arrived.

"Look. What the American planes send to us." He disappeared in back and reappeared immediately with a square of folded paper, incredibly worn and handled, almost ready to come apart where it had been folded. He showed it to us with a portentous look — the line drawing of an ugly, gross pig. Then, winking and giggling at us he unfolded the paper and the drawing became the visage of Adolph Hitler. The old man laughed a shrill eerie laugh.

"See? Hitler... the pig! Dirty swine! See?" He kept folding it back and forth to show how the picture of Hitler folded into the pig and vice versa. We laughed and admired it, wartime propaganda dropped by Allied bombers as they passed deep into Germany. The man had found it, and kept it as a sacred icon. His passion was so strong he still trembled when he held it. One would have thought he'd have lost it many years ago.

We talked a little more, and bought a funnel and a teapot. Then Dorothy asked if he was married...and the light went dead in the old Jew's eyes. A look of uttermost anguish contorted his face.

" I was married. Before the war. You wait, I show you." He disappeared once again into the back and returned with an old, hand crafted hardwood box that had tatters of velvet on the top and mother of pearl inlay along the sides. The top still fitted tightly and he carefully pried it open. Inside were some folded documents and a very old photograph that just fit the box.

It was a sepia-toned family portrait of a man and wife and their four daughters. They were all dressed in their best. He must have been in his early thirties, slim, intense, a little self conscious, and manifestly proud of his family. His wife rested her glossy dark hair against his chest and looked out with a serene gaze. They were seated and kneeling in front of them were their bright-eyed, eager girls, the oldest holding the youngest, and the other two stroking a little black dog.

"My wife...my daughters," he pointed at them with a shaking finger, "All died in the camp. My girls!...all!...all!" His voice was a wail. His chest heaved and he gave an involuntary sob, his mouth working up and down soundlessly.

Dorothy and I were transfixed.

"And see — Pauli!" Sure enough the dog looked a lot like Santos and could have been part schipperke or spitz. Tears had welled up in his eyes and one dropped on the photograph — alarmed, he fumbled for a cloth under the counter and hastened to wipe it, ever so carefully, then dabbed sternly at his eyes. Tears were in my eyes too, as we stood there in the fading afternoon light, tears of sympathy, pathos, and rage at the unspeakable horror perpetrated on that poor old guy; and how a twist of fate, the German economic miracle, rubbed that sad catastrophe in his face every afternoon. Even now, a German group, tipsy from a late liquid luncheon, came barging down the street in high spirits, roaring out a drinking song.

We were silent in communion til the noise moved away and then the heartbroken old tinker looked at Dorth and asked softly, "Why the bambinas? Why?"

22

DESTINY AT DENTON BRIDGE

A full moon rising had turned the muddy waters of Oyster Creek to quicksilver; not so much as a zephyr stirred the surface of the small inlet where our 42-foot gaff ketch Breath lay in the delta of Africa's mighty Gambia River. Just a week ago we had sailed in off a thousand miles of ocean. Snug in this anchorage, landlocked by mud banks and mangroves, we could still hear surf thundering on the bar just beyond the highway bridge.

Santos, our Schipperke lay on the cabin top, forepaws draped over the edge, taking in the powerful scents of West Africa. Santos was a genuine sea dog — born on a boat, given as a five-week puppy to Breath and by now eight years older and 50,000 sea miles wiser. He was a member not only of a family but of a ship's crew. This evening as always, he kept faithful watch from his chosen station on the cabin top, which he vacated only in the worst weather.

Africans had warned us that the Gambia had powerful sorcerers who could easily cast a sleeping spell on our dog, but we retired that night unworried. Santos touched his nose to my wife Dorothy's face as she bent low to nuzzle him goodnight, and his ardent eyes flared briefly — he worshipped his mistress — then he returned to his duty.

We slept easier with him aboard. It was his self-appointed

mission in life to ensure that no one, friend or foe, approached within a 100 yards of Breath without a warning. In truth he was a bit paranoid, but so affectionate to those within his circle that this fault, trifling in a watchdog, was easily forgiven.

Santos made an admirable ship's mascot. His virtues inspired the rest of us — he was brave, selfless, intelligent, passionate, indomitable, as well as dignified, courteous, charming and very lucky. And he represented us vividly to the outside world, creating a dramatic entrance wherever we went ashore, his red harness setting off his jet-black fur as he rode in the very prow of the skiff, like the admiral of hood ornaments.

His noble bearing and unusual looks never failed to attract notice. Without a tail, he'd been mistaken for a peccary, a hedgehog, a Tasmanian devil. When we first landed at Oyster Creek a crowd gathered and a lively debate in Wolof ensued, til one of the policemen from the bridge checkpoint asked in careful English:

"Excuse, sir. What kind of animal that is ?"

"A dog. A boat dog."

"Aha! They think he is baby 'buki'... hyena, sir."

He'd sailed with us up and down the eastern seaboard, through the Caribbean, the Atlantic, and the Mediterranean, keeping sharp watch and good company, and bringing us good luck. In his eight years with us we'd never suffered a mishap.

But tonight, the night of January 3-4, 1991, all that was going to change.

We had come to sail up the Gambia River whose forested banks support a wealth of wildlife — numerous monkeys, a kaleidoscope of birds, hippos, even crocodiles. This chance to see Africa from the deck of our own boat had lured a great crew aboard Breath. Joining Dorothy and me were our sons Diego, 13, and Raffy, 20, along with their young friends Alon and Amos. Dave, my age, took three weeks off from his business in Atlanta for the adventure.

Oyster Creek is a short, navigable waterway that branches off from the Gambia estuary and empties into the Atlantic over an impassable bar at Denton Bridge, several miles down the coastal highway from the city of Banjul. Just before the bridge the creek widens enough to form a good anchorage. Here, Nick, an English sailor who lived in the Gambia offered to let us tie alongside his boat for the night to fill our tanks from his hose ashore. In the morning, with 400 gallons of safe drinking water aboard we would begin our voyage to Basse Santa Su, over 200 miles upriver.

We were sound asleep, just past midnight when our dock lines began to creak. At first I thought a passing boat may have sent a wake, but Santos would have barked at any boat that came by. The creaking got louder. By the time I got on deck to investigate, the ropes had gone from creaking to groaning with stress. Santos was gingerly sniffing at the loudest cleat, bristling his ruff, and expressing his misgivings with a low sporadic growl.

On such a still night there could only be one cause — current. A glance over the side at the small branches speeding past the hull alarmed me — the ebb had tripled its usual spring tide rate. Breath was caught in a freak tidal phenomenon with her long deep keel tied up stern to the stream, the wrong way, like a 20-ton weathervane with its feathers to the wind.

The current took an ever more powerful hold on her keel, determined to wrench it the right way around. The groaning of the lines was turning into shrieks and the cleats on Nick's boat looked ready to snap. Nick appeared on deck distraught. He had never seen such a sudden acceleration of the river before and feared for his boat. His lines were already stretched bar tight to stakes in the bank. If anything gave, both boats would spin off grappled together, helpless to avoid destruction. It was incumbent on me to cast off from Nick, turn Breath around and anchor bow to the stream — right away, before it got any worse.

However, we were in a difficult spot. Just a few boat lengths downstream two high-tension power lines hung across the creek, about 100 ft. apart, carrying the power supply to Serrekunda, the Gambia's biggest town. And close behind them loomed Denton Bridge, a low fixed span resting on massive concrete pillars. If our maneuver went wrong, if we couldn't turn in time, our mainmast might trigger the live wires — we couldn't tell how high they were, but they looked close to the mast top.

And if the boat hit the bridge both masts would be pinned by the roadway while its hull was sucked under and sunk. Just beyond the bridge lay the bar, pounded by heavy surf.

I called everyone up on deck to move the boat. As they hurried topsides Santos sensed something wrong. Why was his mistress up and about after midnight? Why was she starting the engine at this hour? Why was the normally bantering crew so quiet? He stood by, poised to react.

We cast off the lines, and hung briefly to a stern anchor we had set that afternoon as a safety. Tethered from her stern, Breath yawed violently out into the stream, and then veered back again, almost hitting boats to either end of her giddy arc.

The anchor was dragging, but very slowly. We had time to try motoring hard astern while my strong crew hauled on the line. Hopefully we could work the boat backwards to gain more room from boats moored nearby to make our turn. We needed it; Breath's long straight keel and heavy displacement were more suited to making long steady runs on the high seas than sharp turns in constricted waterways.

We succeeded taking in rope but most of it smoked out of my crew's hands when they went to cleat it. It writhed against the teak bitts and screeched like an animal in agony. Santos, eager to play a part, hovered around the boys' heels til he got tripped on, and added his sharp yelp to the rope's shriek.

"Come here Santos!" called Dorothy, a center of calm sitting in the cockpit as shouts flew overhead and bodies lurched back and forth. She held him in her lap and tried to soothe him. He was quivering with excitement, eager to act.

Again we won and lost rope in the struggle to cleat it without crushing a finger. Then, as the boat sheered out from shore, the rope ran amok. In rapid succession it pinned Dave against the mizzen shrouds, almost nipped Alon's thumb off against the cleat, jumped to the rudder head and threatened to break it off till Raff, making a dangerous leap, wrested it free.

My friend Marco sprang to mind — one-legged Marco, whose thigh had been caught in a coil and instantly severed while docking a ferry in strong winds. Our own line was out of control. If it snapped, its backlash might take an eye, even a life. We needed to be free of it. I shouted, "Cast off the anchor line!" and out it snaked, irretrievable.

I gunned the engine into a turn and almost turned the boat around but the current ran even swifter near the middle of the stream and suddenly threatened to skewer us on the sharp steel bow of a derelict racing yacht moored there. I steered to go around behind it but halfway into the turn realized we were going to hit the wire. In desperation I steered back towards the bank where the wire rose to the pylon. Dorothy clutched the dog and we all held our breath.

We just tipped it. There was flare of blue flame, a meteor shower of sparks and we were through, unharmed — but the second wire was coming up fast — and directly behind it loomed up the stone bridge. I flung the helm over hard and jack-hammered the diesel but we struck anyway — a long, scraping skid, the top six inches of our mainmast pinned hard against the power line.

40,000 volts exploded down the shrouds, hideous incandescence lit up the sky, and a powerful hissing roar filled the air. Time stopped. Transfixed, we watched welding fires flare every four feet down the mainstay. Flames leapt up inside the cabin, the switchboard spewed molten aluminum, fuses shot from their sockets, and smoke began to billow out the hatches.

Cars on the highway screeched to a stop. Police came sprinting from the checkpoint across the bridge. Nick stood rooted in horror to his deck, while Louis, his wizened, grouchy old watchman, sobbed, "Boss! They're dying! They're dying!" All watched as blue fire glowed about the rig like a deadly spirit. No sound came from the boat save the crackle of electrocution.

Suddenly the fireworks stopped. The cable had rolled over the mast top, and now we were headed down a perilously narrow corridor, between the second wire and the bridge, towards the far bank, which was looming up inexorably. We had turned enough, the top of the mast pivoting against the wire, to be facing the current, so I had control of the boat — but we had no way out. We were boxed in between the wire and the bridge.

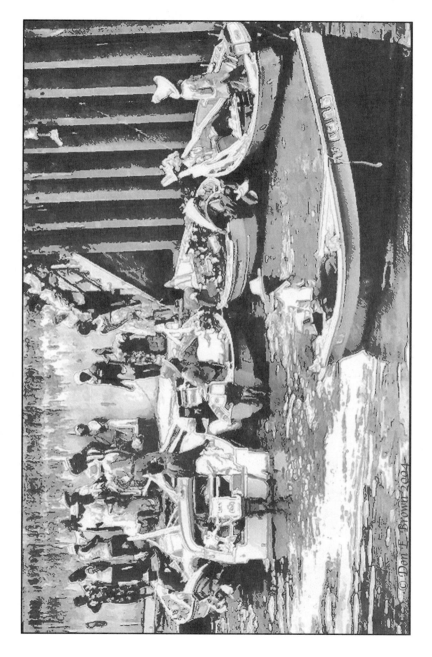

For a long moment we were frozen, between worlds, unable to speak; even irrepressible Santos was stunned into silence. People watching from the shore, seeing no movement, hearing no sound, assumed now that we had been killed. Then, from the foredeck, Dave gave a shout.

"Watch out for the wire — it's close!"

Santos immediately wriggled out of Dorothy's arms and dashed up to the action.

Dorothy addressed the boys, almost casually. "Fire. Fire below...get the extinguishers." They flung themselves down the hatches to blast everything that moved with dry chemical.

I couldn't see the wires because the awning was still up. Guided by shouts, I brought her carefully around in that narrow aisle, afraid to hit the wire but absolutely terrified of hitting the pilings with our rudder. We proceeded back towards the other bank, minds racing, wondering what to do. We were trapped. There was nowhere to go but back out — through the wire. We'd survived it once; we'd have to brave it again.

The wheel hard over, the throttle full blast we braced for impact. The mast top hit the cable, erupting like a volcano, sending a torrent of fat red sparks to the deck. They floated down like fallout from a giant sparkler. Dave ducked back under the shelter of the awning but Santos, eyes fixed ahead, stayed to defend the foredeck. He was still growling for all he was worth when the fiery rain of electrified harmattan dust landed in his fur. Uttering a high-pitched scream, Santos sprinted down the side deck with cinders glowing in his coat, panic in his eyes, and plunged into the water. When he surfaced he was already swimming with all his might for the boat, his paws pumping the water at a desperate rate, his eyes fastened on Dorothy — but the current swept him away.

There wasn't a thing we could do for him. An instant later, a blast like a small thunderbolt arc-welded the mainstay just four feet above where Amos had instinctively grabbed it for balance. His body contorted, arched backwards and disappeared over the side into the river. Raffy, at the forward shrouds, flipped backwards off the foredeck. I was flung back hard against the mizzenmast. We felt the cold quiver of AC voltage tingling in our cells. Directly behind us loomed the stone pillars of the bridge, mere feet away from the vulnerable rudder. The night was on fire; the boat was on fire!

Then we were through...off the wire...engine hammering steadily in the quiet night air. Diego and Alon seized their fire extinguishers and again attacked the flames, as I steered towards safety.

In the water, Raff — a Dartmouth swimmer — struck out for the bank, swimming for his life, and barely made it to shore as the current tried to pull him out to sea. Amos spread-eagled himself against a bridge piling and was rescued by Nick in his motorized dinghy.

Against all odds we were safe and sound — all the humans at least. But there was no sign of Santos. Dave and Raffy went that night to call for the dog along both shores, but drew a blank. Dorothy and Diego were out the next morning early, searching well down the coast, til the African sun blazing onto the empty beach drove them back.

Still there was hope.... an old fisherman mending his nets told Alon that the current had probably set south at well over a knot. The ebb tide had started around midnight, and went six hours before reversing. We measured it off on the chart. If he was right, Santos could have been carried 6 miles down the coast by dawn — to Cape St. Mary, a long bulge of coastline marked by white sand beaches and a number of tourist hotels.

We were hard at work cleaning and repairing the boat when Dorothy put on her walking shoes and said,

"I hate to leave you with this shambles, but I won't rest easy til I've searched around Cape St. Mary. Maybe at one of the hotels. Somebody must have seen him!" She gave me a crooked smile and set out with Alon.

They took a transport to Cape St. Mary and walked for miles down the beach, making inquiries at every hotel. She went from the Sunwing to the Senegambia, talking to beach attendants, tourists, vendors; but nobody had seen or heard of a little black dog. Finally, tired and dejected, they sat on a high dune overlooking the sea and faced the likelihood that he hadn't survived — or that if he had, we might never find him. Somehow that seemed worse. Dorothy started to cry and soon Alon too was blinking back the tears.

Yet she came back persistent — offering a reward over the radio, notifying the Denton Bridge police, and nailing up handprinted signs on trees and telephone poles. She asked Samba Sey, a young Gambian who made a living as a yacht agent, to put the word out along the coast and to keep his eyes open.

It was touching, but it seemed futile. In plain view beyond the bridge was the Oyster Creek bar, broad flats of hard sand on which pounded row after row of breakers. They mounted up like penitentiary walls, massive, forbidding, collapsing with such force that they sent tremors through the earth. The mental image of Santos funneled helplessly into that cauldron made me wince. True, we'd lost him before and he'd always turned up, but this time everybody except Dorothy assumed a shark must have found his battered corpse.

When we had repaired the damage it was time to leave Oyster Creek, if we wanted to cruise upriver before meeting a deadline in the Virgin Islands. Santos still hadn't turned up. Though he'd never been gone more than a day or two before, Dorothy clung to the hope that her dog would appear unexpectedly.

"Honey," I pleaded, "We've got to get on with our life...do the river, cross the Atlantic, get back to work."

"But what if he survived?" she said. "He was such a strong swimmer. What if he somehow finds his way back here — and we're gone!"

"I find it hard to believe he survived that surf," I said flatly. "And then swam til dawn." I didn't mention sharks to her.

"Mom," said Raff gently. "I hate to say it but I think Dad's right. Amos and I went out at slack tide...that day...to see if we could surf those breakers. No way! Would have broken our necks." Amos nodded agreement somberly.

"Surely we would be the first to hear if he had made it," Dave added. "He was the most distinctive damn dog I ever seen, and y'all put out the word for him up and down the coast. And the reward — a month's pay for a workin' man here — you think they ain't been scouring the bushes for him?"

That stopped her. There was a painful silence as she searched our faces, looking for a reprieve from reality. Then her eyes flooded, her shoulders shook, and her voice broke.

"I just didn't want to abandon hi-hi-him —!" Tears were rolling down her cheeks. Her agitated sons hugged her, Alon and Amos turned away embarrassed, and Dave gripped my shoulder, concern creasing his face. Next morning, with heavy hearts, we hauled the anchor for our long-awaited trip upriver.

Our loss really hit home at a side creek 50 miles upriver where we were anchored awaiting a favorable tide. Suddenly we saw a strange face peering in at the porthole inquiring politely if we wanted to buy a fish. The fisherman had paddled up silently alongside in a dugout. When Santos was alive that could never have happened. Now we sorely missed the zealous barking we'd so often tried to hush.

And again, the next day when Dorothy and I returned from buying bread in the village, the skiff was tied behind the boat, and the guys were all down below playing whist and listening to rock and roll. We stood in the dust and the sun calling in vain for a ride til one of the boys happened to come on deck and hear us. Santos would have shrilled the alarm for his mistress even before she got to the riverbank.

Not a day went by without someone bringing up another Santos story. What an amazing little character he had been! We'd never see another like him, I thought.

One night I woke to an empty bed, got up, and found Dorothy sitting in the moonlight. From the way her eyes glistened I could tell she'd been thinking of Santos.

I sat down and put an arm around her. After a while she spoke.

"You know what I miss most? His shaggy mane filling the porthole. He liked to watch me cook. Now every time a shadow falls over that port it reminds me of the love in those bright black eyes... I miss his little spirit."

"He was as noble in spirit as any person," I said. "Maybe that's what makes me wonder... "

"Wonder what?"

"Well.... do you realize how incredibly lucky we were? Both our boys could have been killed. Can you imagine calling Alon's or Amos' folks — to tell them their only son just died? God help us! So many things could have taken our lives, but we all survived — unscathed! It's ...it's too... somebody had to die...!'"

"Huh?"

"Blame it on my religious upbringing but I keep seeing Santos as a kind of sacrificial lamb. A bold, warlike one. He gave us all of his luck, then took our place in the jaws of death. Rendered his greatest service at the very end of his life — what a way to check out!"

We watched the moon slip below the treetops.

"Farfetched...." said my wife sleepily, "But it's a comforting thought."

Two weeks had passed, and we had made our way 150 miles up the Gambia to Georgetown. We still had no word of Santos, nor did we expect any. On another calm, bone dry, hazy savanna day Breath was anchored near a large tree overhanging the river. Dorothy and I were reinforcing the awning and watching monkeys cavort while the boys played a boisterous game of whist at the table in the main saloon.

Suddenly I heard an engine. I looked up and saw a yacht motoring upriver, the first we'd seen since Banjul. It was a catamaran flying Italian colors. When they saw us they steered across the river to come near, inspecting us with binoculars before hailing us.

"Hello...are you the Americans that lost the little black dog?"

"Yes...?" I said, cautiously. The whist game below went dead silent.

"I don't say if it is yours, but Samba say that tell you — the police at Denton Bridge have a small black dog was found on the beach."

For a couple of seconds we were struck speechless — then

a wave of incredulous joy broke over the boat and the entire crew tumbled up on deck shouting "Oh my God yes! YES!"

Could it possibly be? It had to be! Dorothy and I immediately resolved to return to the coast but before we left I cautioned the crew.

"Remember, someone might easily have found a stray mutt that was black and brought it in, hoping for the reward. Don't get your hopes too high."

We set off well before dawn the next morning, crossing the river by silent dugout, listening as the birds awoke and began to call. An ancient school bus, rusted to the bone, took us past a couple miles of desolate bush to the central road, where an erratic series of transports took us the rest of the way.

At long last we rolled into Banjul. With hope and trepidation we caught a taxi to the bridge to see if Santos had truly survived. The police officer on duty greeted us warmly.

"You have come for your dog!" he announced then turned and called peremptorily, "Small boy! Go to fisherman Ceesay's compound and tell him bring the dog!" A ten-year-old barefoot lad who'd been hanging around the door dashed off with the summons. We spoke with the officer, who had been on duty that fateful night, and waited on tenterhooks to see the dog.

Then, there he was, unquestionably Santos, coming down the path from the highway, led on a ratty piece of polypropylene string. He seemed listless, and he walked with a limp, his head held down. But when Dorothy dropped to her knees and called "Santos!" she flicked the power back on. His head shot up, his ears snapped forward, his eyes caught fire, his whole body trembled — as that beloved voice registered. Then, like a jet catapulted off a carrier's deck, he leapt into her arms and covered her hands and face with quick, deft licks, squirming with delight. Dorothy buried her face in his thick ruff and hugged him a long time.

This time, when she looked up, the tears in her eyes were a balm to my heart.

The police officer told us that early the morning after we had hit the wires, a Swedish tourist staying at the Sunwing

Hotel, five miles from Denton Bridge, was walking the beach looking for birds, and found Santos. The Swede deduced the obvious — that Santos must have fallen off some vessel. He smuggled Santos back into his hotel room and fed him. Thus Santos was at the Sunwing that afternoon when Dorothy arrived to inquire if anyone had seen a small black dog. Nobody had — the Swede had been careful when he violated the hotel rules. When he had to fly home, he gave Santos to the police who gave him to a fisherman to keep until we might return. They also notified Samba, the self-appointed yacht agent, who passed the word to the Italian catamaran.

We spent that night in a Banjul hotel, Santos sleeping blissfully in Dorothy's arms. We noticed his hair had turned white about the muzzle, and when we patted him on his right flank he sometimes yelped with a spasm of pain. We wondered what he had experienced, as he was swept into the maelstrom of breakers, then out to sea and five miles down the coast. We marveled at his fortitude and his luck. But most of all we were grateful to have him back.

It took all the next day and into the dark before we finally got to the big tree by the river whose roots served as a landing stage for our dinghy. We could see the lights of the boat, so I gave a shout for the boys and heard their answering blast on the conch horn.

"Do you have him? Did you find Santos?" they called. Dorothy urged the dog to bark. His unmistakable voice rang across the calm river and a cheer of wild exuberance bounced back over the glossy water.

Santos resumed his place in the crew uncowed by his narrow escape. A week after his return we were 200 miles upstream exploring a jungle-choked creek. Rowing and drifting in the skiff, we surprised a troop of baboons sunning themselves on a dead branch overhanging the water. True to form, Santos leapt straight off the bow, a bloodcurdling growl in his throat, and surfaced swimming full tilt. The baboons grudgingly moved into the forest, flinging many a scornful backward glance at our fiery dog, as we headed him off for his own safety with an oar.

That night, back on Breath, a solitary baboon gave a hoarse bark from the riverside forest. Santos bristled with affront and hurled back a piercing retort. In unison the whole baboon clan erupted with a howl of invective, which Santos returned lustily, bouncing stiff-legged off the deck with each passionate bark. For a moment uproar filled the fragrant air; then silence drifted back in.

We praised our fiery dog for upholding Breath's honor and then retired to our bunks, leaving Santos back on station, forepaws draped over the cabin top, once again keeping his watch over the night.

23.

THE PARROT

One natural wonder followed hard on the heels of another along the northern rim of the South American continent.

I sailed past deserts, snow capped mountains and jungles still stalked by jaguars...explored wrecks, ruins, famous cities — but my favorite memory after I returned home was of a parrot on the little Dutch island of Bonaire.

I had arrived there after spending weeks alone anchored behind a long barrier reef. Starved for company, I wandered about the quiet streets of Kralendijk and entered every shop looking more for conversation than for something to buy. Eventually I entered an unlikely looking dry goods store, thinking I might find some canvas.

I looked around the dimly lit interior. The air was stuffy, a little musty — the store looked like it had remained unchanged for half a century.

The sales lady stood behind an old wooden counter at the far end of the room. When I spoke to her she seemed not to hear. I tried again, went up to her, and asked for canvas. She knit her brows furiously, searched her stock, then pulled out a bolt of something flimsy with flowers on it. I had to say no; she grimaced, taking it personally.

Then I heard an unmistakable squawk and noticed a parrot in a wire cage on a counter right near by. It was an amazon, mostly green with a bright yellow head. It opened the gate with its beak, waddled out and climbed straight to the top of the cage where it gave a screech for attention.

When I asked her, this time in Spanish, if the bird talked, her face's defenses fell away. She told me, animatedly, not only did the parrot talk, it could carry on a conversation over the telephone — and it could sing the national anthem.

The bird stepped carefully on to her wrist, and rapidly sidled up to her shoulder where it stood on one foot then the other, the eyes surging red with emotion. Then the little old lady cocked her head sideways towards the parrot, the parrot cocked its head towards hers til they almost touched, and they began to sing together the national anthem of Bonaire.

I stood there spellbound, watching the happiness in the old woman's eyes and the joy bursting out of the little green bird as it sang away on her shoulder.

The parrot not only had all the lyrics memorized, but it sounded just like its mistress, mimicking her voice right down to every crack and quaver. The accuracy of the rendition — so loving, so faithful, belted out in that raucous parrot timbre — was uncanny and endearing, not to mention comic in the extreme. I couldn't stop laughing. The old lady was laughing too, and beaming with pride, and the parrot laughed just the way she did.

Over the years that image of the parrot and the little old lady became one of the stories I told my daysail guests back on St. John. People often said that it would be perfect for the funniest animal videos program on TV.

So a decade or two later, I once again closed with Bonaire, rode the swift current around its southern tip, then steered a stone's throw from its leeward coast up towards Kralendijk past houses built on the low seaside bluffs that became more and more numerous, til we arrived at the anchorage off town. Even here the water was crystal clear.

I went ashore to the customs house. After clearing the boat in I asked the young officer if he knew of a lady who had a parrot, a remarkable bird that could sing the national anthem. He immediately said "Oh yes! That is a famous bird in this island. It can talk...really talk."

"Does she still work at the dry goods store?" I asked.

"You'll have to ask at the store." He pointed up the street.

In the years since I'd been there, new buildings had sprouted up, and old ones had been remodeled. Gift shops selling the piquant and the charming had replaced the old mom and pop stores selling necessities. Prime among the casualties of the new order was Miss Yeta's shop. Now it was airy, well-lit, filled with customers — and the management sat on a raised platform where they could keep a sharp eye on the door.

"Oh ... Miss Yeta you mean. She's retired now. She used to run the store — years back — and yes she still has Clara. That bird is almost human. It can talk, you know...and it won first place in the animal exhibition."

We asked around. People repeated stories about Clara and Miss Yeta traveling to Curacao and how the parrot talked to people it knew over the phone. I wondered; could this bird actually talk? I knew gorillas had been taught to spell a number of words. Perhaps this exceptional bird could speak to the point — not just "parrot" the words.

The next day we rented a Suzuki and toured the island. When we got back we were cruising slowly through town when a car pulled abreast and its driver, a young man in his twenties, waved us down, shouting. Miss Yeta's nephew had found us. Kralendijk was a small town and word of gringos with a video camera had made the rounds.

We first stocked up with fruit, then followed our guide down a narrow paved road that ran straight as an arrow through scrub cactus, before we turned off on a dirt road that sent up a plume of dust heralding our passage.

Finally we came to a dwelling — a small house with concrete walls, and an extensive galvanized roof that shaded a large open area that had a table and some easy chairs. An impenetrable fence of interlocking century plants fortified by ranks of dildo cactus kept livestock out of her front yard — where laundry lay strewn to the sun on a cactus bush whose thorns pinned down the sheets to keep them from billowing away in the stiff breeze.

Even though she had agreed to be filmed, Miss Yeta seemed nervous about the video camera. Whenever she saw it pointing her way she frowned. And Clara, far from appreciating the feast of fruit we'd brought, stood on the table and screeched something at us over and over again.

"Vapa kaz! Vapa kaz!"

Finally Miss Yeta calmed it down long enough to sing a bit of the Bonairean anthem and snatches of Happy Birthday in English and Spanish. Clara ate some banana, but savaged the grapefruit and flung it scornfully off the table. It threatened to bite any hand that came too close when we tried to hand feed it. Especially when we filmed Miss Yeta it carried on like a soul possessed: calling, whistling and shrieking. Miss Yeta, looking ill at ease, tried to shush it without success.

"Vapa kaz vapa kaz."

"What's she saying?" I finally asked the nephew. He looked sheepish and said, "She saying 'Va pa cas.' It is in our language, Papiamento."

"What does it mean?" I persisted.

"It mean 'Go to home! Go home!' Funny parrot..."

Suddenly I remembered that certain societies in Africa do not appreciate having their pictures taken and wondered if Miss Yeta, age 79, was feeling dubious about the sudden descent of a carful of foreign white people with their long-snouted video camera focused like some kind of star wars weapon.

I decided it was time to end our little visit and so we left, thanking Miss Yeta, taking our leave of her formidable animal, who as we drove away could still be heard, triumphant, "Va pa cas! Va pa cas!"

So it could really talk after all.

24.

ANOTHER ISLAND...ANOTHER LIBRARY

I dropped anchor off the town in three fathoms and wiped the crystallized salt off my face, wondering whether Nevis even had a library, much less anything worth such a wet trip. Ashore the island's capitol dozed under a patchwork of rusty roofing. All was quiet save the bleating of goats being loaded onto a slab-sided sailing lighter bound for nearby St. Kitts.

A bucolic venue for a book search, yet sometimes the sleepiest backwaters had the most interesting volumes from the previous century, that had sat prominent, if unread, in a plantation great house til its owner went blind from too much jack iron rum, or died, and they ended up in the town library.

As it turned out, not only was there a library, but it was located above the courthouse, in the heart of town — which was more impressive seen from close up, its substantial buildings of cut stone testifying to a distant prosperity.

And there was a serious librarian, an old-fashioned West Indian lady in a suit of grey wool, who regarded my T-shirt and flip-flops dubiously — making me glad I had changed into long pants before I went ashore. I told her I was pursuing the 16th century in a small boat, sailing island to island, library to library.

"To what purpose?" she asked, her face softening.

" I ask myself that a lot...for some reason the era has always fascinated me."

189

Apparently she approved. She led me over well-worn, creaky hardwood floors to a table under a lethargic ceiling fan and unlocked a bookshelf cased with chicken wire. "Look on the second shelf," she said as she left.

There, bound in old leather, with only traces of its gilt lettering left, a volume beckoned to me. I extricated it carefully, blew off a film of dust, and started reading. First published in 1827!

Outside the window two iron cannons stood guard over a small square below, where chickens scratched and a hedge shouted red hibiscus at the top of its lungs. Beyond, Nevis Peak towered alone, scarcely changed since Columbus sailed past. In its long shadow five centuries melted away, and the book took me back to a turbulent time of desperate voyages, insurrections, shipwrecks, and treasure.

That's how I first heard about Cubagua, the small desert island between Isla Margarita and the Venezuelan mainland. In a few brief entries C. T. Southey's Chronological History of the West Indies told about the attacks by Caribs and corsairs on the lawless, wealthy boomtown at Cubagua, where brutally enslaved Indians dived up a fabulous fortune in pearls. A terrific story featuring free diving and sailing, which I loved — and I'd never heard a word about it!

I searched, as best I could — living on a remote cay in the US Virgins long before the Internet — for more about Cubagua. The Encyclopedia Britannica had two lines about it. Nothing in the St. Thomas libraries mentioned it.

Time passed. I built a larger boat and crossed the Atlantic to Spain with my family. We wintered in Seville, home of the famous Archivos General de las Indias — if any place held the answers to Cubagua it would be the AGI.

With my researcher's pass in hand I passed between the heavy black chains that ringed the building, through the stone portals, ascended the marble staircase, pushed open the tall double doors — and found myself, awed, in the AGI's reading room. Here I worked at a lustrous mahogany table on a chair ornate with polished brass while attendants in dark suits brought me original parchment documents, some stained by salt water, others singed, wax seal and blotting sand still clinging to the pages. The only problem...I could scarcely read a word of the Cubagua folio.

I consulted an acquaintance, a genial white-haired professor on sabbatical from a university in Uruguay. He perused a couple of pages, chuckling as he tamped his pipe.

"No wonder...I can hardly read it myself. Spanish was very different in the early 1500's...like Chaucer's English. But the AGI receives copies of any book whose authors did research here. Look in that card catalogue," he said.

Within minutes I had found Enrique Otte's recently published, exhaustively researched account of Cubagua, "Las Perlas del Caribe," printed in modern Spanish. I spent the next week absorbing what there was to know about Cubagua.

....

Isla Cubagua offered no gold, no inhabitants to enslave, not even any fresh water — but off its coasts oysters grew in profusion. After an expedition in 1499 returned to Spain with a hundredweight of pearls, word spread like wildfire; Cubagua became the New World's first boom town.

At first the Spaniards traded with the Indians for pearls but soon figured out they needed, not partners, but slaves who could be driven hard in the race for profit.

The perfect slaves for Cubagua came from the Bahamas, the Lucayan Indians, exceptional divers — indeed exceptional people, noted for their physical and their spiritual beauty by the likes of Columbus, Ponce de Leon and Las Casas. Columbus added crassly that they would be easy to enslave.

Crass...but prophetic. The first slavers told the Lucayos that they had come from the spirit world to take them to visit their dead loved ones. The trusting souls swarmed eagerly aboard ship, the hatches were clamped shut, and the ship sailed them — to join their relatives soon enough, it is true. The Lucayos were dived to death. Sharks took many and exhaustion took the rest.

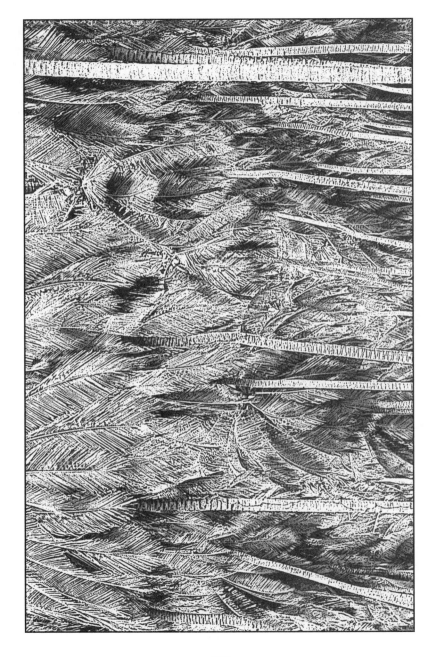

By 1520, Cubagua was reeling out of control. Drinking, brawling, murder and rape finally provoked the Indians to a furious insurrection, killing all Spaniards they could catch and driving out the rest.

But not for long. The Christians returned in force, exacted grim revenge, and rebuilt. Nueva Cadiz de Cubagua rose on the ashes of the previous settlement, this time with stone walls, polished floors, glass windows and lace trimmings — even a convent and a brothel. For a moment, it was the finest Spanish town in the New World.

Then, as suddenly as it had begun, Cubagua's boom went bust. The supply of oysters dwindled drastically. The pious claimed God had finally revenged himself on the town's wickedness, while others blamed a disease brought on by over-fishing. Eventually Cubagua reverted back to its original state.

....

After we returned to the Caribbean I did a couple of deliveries through the Bahamas, and looked at the Lucayans' islands with heightened interest. That such innocent, beautiful people living in such lovely surroundings should have suffered a fate so horrible —- it woke me shouting more nights than one.

Finally I sailed to Cubagua. We arrived in a glassy calm — perfect pearl-diving weather. Or was it? Within the short space of half an hour we saw three big hammerhead sharks cruising at the surface, one with the girth of an ox, which made an evil lunge at our dinghy. Odd — in twenty years of sailing the Caribbean I'd seen a shark fin at the surface once, in the distance. Here in half an hour I'd seen three...right next to the boat. I'm not superstitious, at least not for a sailor, but given my fascination with the fate of the Lucayans, it seemed a remarkable coincidence.

The next morning my son and I walked across desolate cracked mud flats towards the ruins of Nueva Cadiz. Not a soul was around. Then, just as we neared the coral rock ruins, we came across a singular sight — a human skeleton, half buried, with an iron spearhead lodged deep between its ribs. It looked like it had been exposed by a transient downpour that had eroded a shallow gully in the sandy soil. The blade was incredibly pitted, but whole. I stood there, amazed by this second coincidence, feeling a sense of déjà vu while the mountains that overlooked Cubagua seemed to loom into my focus. Barren and brooding, they conveyed anguish frozen in stone.

I stood there, reluctant to move lest I break the spell, and found myself entertaining thoughts about...well...reincarnation. Logically, the idea of many lives is not such a stretch. That we are here at all, right now – that's what's amazing. Having been here once, why not once again?

Was it possible that those sharks, this skeleton... ...

"Dad...you OK? You look kinda spaced," interrupted my son, quizzical.

Reality came belting back down with the heat. My head cleared, we explored the ruins for awhile and then returned to the boat, grateful for its shade and ice water.

When we sailed away. I gave Cubagua a long last look. I felt a sense of completion. Why, I wasn't quite sure... but it was enough.

25.

A LIGHTHOUSE TO LOVE

Approaching Puerto Rico by sea on a clear, moonless night I gradually became aware of an immense loom of light rising up from the densely populated island. As my vessel closed with the coast, individual lights began to appear – the powerful airport beacon revolving a searchlight into the sky, then stadium lights, and eventually the one I was looking for – the 10-second flash of the lighthouse on El Morro, the magnificent fortress that was built to protect San Juan harbor.

All night long that precisely charted light guided shipping in and out of the busy port – a constant flow of container ships, oil tankers, bulk carriers, huge car transports, inter-island traders, yachts like me, tugs with tows, fishing boats, and cruise ships, called "birthday cakes" by sailors since they blaze with light.

When morning came, I was close enough to shore to make out the long defensive wall of Old San Juan leading to El Morro. As I glided past its ramparts, I spotted the lighthouse, looking like a Moorish tower – the oldest lighthouse on the island. It begged an exploration.

Once the boat was safely anchored, my wife and I crossed the waterfront boulevard that runs noisy with trucks and then the old town closed in around us... near the docks a demi-monde of seedy hole-in-the-wall bars seemed to blink uncomfortably in the bright daylight, being more at ease in shadows late of nights when transvestites and prostitutes gather looking for seamen.

Away from the docks well-restored buildings from previous centuries lined cobblestone walkways. Pastry shops sold elegant confections and strong coffee, pensioners sat in pocket plazas on park benches feeding a flock of pigeons and gazing out to the harbor below. Second and third story balconies with graceful black iron railings and flowerboxes over-spilling with colorful blossoms lifted the gaze of passersby, like us, who spent most of the afternoon in art galleries and bookshops, meandering happily towards the lighthouse.

Puerto Rico is, to those of us who live in the eastern Caribbean, the center. When we need plane connections to the rest of the world, or specialized medical treatment, or a hard-to-find part we automatically turn to San Juan. It's the biggest and the best til Miami. Befitting a metropolis its coast boasts 14 major lighthouses, architectural treasures built in Spanish colonial times, each one presiding over its portion of the island.

Some people choose to learn about an island through its music. Others visit its museums, still others its taverns. For me, a lifelong sailor, lighthouses are my reference point. They guide me into harbor and help shape my experience ashore. In Puerto Rico, each one is a step in a quest for the isle the Indians called Borinquen.

. . . .

The Coast Guard jet came out of nowhere, traveling faster than its sound. For an instant we glimpsed tons of machinery hurtling low over the water, silent as an apparition. Then the shriek of its engine broke over us like a tsunami of sound, a ripping, tearing thunderclap that was gone as fast as it had come.

A voice came over the radio "Yacht Breath, where are you headed?"

"To Rincon, PR."

© Don E. Brown 2004

"We've got unconfirmed report of an overturned boat with people clinging to it. Keep a sharp lookout please, and call the Coast Guard on channel 16 if you see anything."

"That's a roger."

All night we watched but saw nothing. Had another boatload of illegal aliens drowned? Eventually we picked up the Rincon light and steered for it, wondering how many "yolas" were homing in on it with us — "yolas" being the marginal, overloaded boats that wait at the western edge of the Mona Passage for good weather before setting out with their hopeful human cargo.

I had a good friend living near Rincon, Don, who met us and drove us past the lighthouse, which has been made into a park. I thought of the contrast between the surfers and beach potatoes soaking up sun — and the aliens just over the horizon intent on running their "yolas" aground and scattering into anonymity.

"You should have been here last week," exclaimed Don. "A big drop of Dominicans hit my beach around one in the morning — they favor me because this is the largest piece of vacant property on this coast. People were running by, shadows coming out of shadows, scrambling through the bush. I heard a banging on my door, opened it pistol in hand and found a woman collapsed on the step. ... Must of been 6 months pregnant. She asked me for water and I gave her a gallon jug out of the fridge, and went to call a doctor — but she was gone when I got off the phone."

....

Lighthouse maintenance does not exactly top the list of priorities in Haiti. Sailing along that coast one never knows if a given light will be working, or a buoy on station. We had sailed a cargo of medical supplies from the VI to Haiti and were returning via a long tack offshore. We had never even sighted the DR, when we picked up the Cabo Rojo light. We were still well beyond its nominal range, and the contrast it posed with the dim or nonexistent lights of Haiti dramatized the difference between the richest and the poorest nations in the hemisphere.

The Cabo Rojo light is set on a flat rock peninsula at the SW and opposite end of the island from San Juan, in an attractive, rural part of the island. Nearby to the east is the famous La Parguera lagoon, so charged and volatile with phosphorescence that even small fish leave trails like comets. To the north lies the bottle green bay of Boqueron, one of the most pleasant anchorages in Puerto Rico. Here we dropped anchor and gave our voyage a pause.

Ashore a quaint wooden town lined the main drag, which made a sudden turn for the interior leaving behind it a long broad beach backed by well kept coconut trees with white-washed bases. Behind the town, green pastures and rolling hills led to the western cordillera.

We wandered the main street and ended up in the plaza where street vendors sold oysters, winking knowingly and making appropriate gestures as they sold me these reputed aphrodisiacs. As I sat eating, sharing with my wife — after all one hand can't clap — up came a magnificent stallion, a proud handsome youth riding it right up the main street. Soon he was joined by two more horsemen, on fine mounts and richly-tooled leather saddles. The ringing beat of horses' hooves against old cobblestones reminded me of the stately era that had preceded highways and traffic jams, that had deliberately built the old lighthouse to be more pleasing to the eye than a steel pole and a transformer behind a chain link fence.

. . . .

It was an ugly night on the high seas and I desperately wanted to know — exactly — where we were. We'd left Venezuela four days ago, in my 42-foot ketch. The forecast had been favorable until this afternoon when the Coast Guard broadcast had warned of a rapidly developing tropical depression that would begin affecting us by noon tomorrow. If I knew just what course to steer I could probably beat the storm to Bahia

Jobos, on the south coast of Puerto Rico where winding channels amid mangrove labyrinths offered immunity from any weather. But my GPS was broken and the heavy overcast had precluded sextant sights. Where was I really? A 30-mile error in my estimated position was not inconceivable.

Around midnight a thunderbolt nailed the sea in front of us like a welding torch. Instantly followed a dreadful crack of thunder. Not a soul aboard but longed for land as we crashed along, sending up gouts of spray in the wretched night. More lightning was on its way when low on the horizon ahead I saw a faint sweep of light...and again... the Punta Tuna light.

I plotted its bearing on the chart and set a course for Jobos. We made it just after dawn, and motored up the channel til all sight of the horizon was cut off by the mangrove forest. There we anchored and took lines to the trees, then I spent most of the day sleeping through the howling squalls.

Lighthouses are easy to love.

Once the weather had blown by I went by "publico" to Punta Tuna. Publicos are group taxis and a Puerto Rican traditional transport that connects one town to the next. In each town you catch another one going your way... When there are no more publicos you are there.

I found myself in a vintage Ford that swayed around the curves of a country road, ran high above the sparkling sea and dipped down into villages where fishing boats were pulled up on beaches, their nets hung to dry.

Sometimes it veered inland between rows of flamboyant trees in heat, their interlocking canopies ablaze with red flowers. It sped by houses with bright gardens, occasionally let someone out at a "colmado," a small roadside grocery store where men played dominoes and drank cerveza in dense shade beneath a mango tree.

I walked the last stretch to where I could drink in the details of the lighthouse. It sits solidly on a rocky point, Puerto Rico's southeast thrust into the Caribbean Sea. Its bluff base and intrepid tower, stoutly built out of stone, declared that no matter what storms might blow, the Punta Tuna light would always send its double flash forth into the dark night. Somehow that was a comfort in this often-dark world of man....

26.

INTERLUDE AT INAGUA

The boat floated motionless on a sea of blue light, on a flat calm morning in the Windward Passage. The only land in sight was Haiti, 30 miles off, its peaks etched in smoky lavender atop the cloudless horizon. The crew slept. All was quiet on board save for the occasional slap of a wavelet or the creak of the gaff saddle against the mast. A distant drone, perhaps a bumblebee wandered far from land, made itself barely audible. Then, as if in a dream, the drone began to accelerate, louder, closer, faster than we could comprehend.

Suddenly, falling out of nowhere, a terrifying shriek ripped the sky. Hearts pounding we tumbled up on deck just in time to glimpse a white jet with a red stripe hurtle low over the water very close behind our boat. For an instant it seemed to stop, we could see the pilot's goggles watching us, and then it flung off, leaving roar and smoke and bleeding air behind, to become once again a distant drone high in the sky — the US Coast Guard patrolling its salt fief.

Silence filtered back in and our adrenalin was beginning to subside when a helicopter clattered out of the west and took up station 50 ft. off our stern, so out of place and unexpected as to seem a hallucination, but deafening. It hung there for five full minutes, its twin missiles aimed at our cockpit, its downdraft buffeting the blue sea into angry froth. We felt like peasants face down in a rice paddy.

When it peeled off our VHF came alive. On the horn was a Coast Guard cutter with a lengthy interrogation. I told them we were a family of four, with a friend, headed for Great Inagua on our 42-foot gaff ketch, and that our last port had been Kingston.

"Kingston...Jamaica?" — an undisguised tremor of interest in the wooden voice.

"That's affirmative."

A long pause. When the voice came back it was brisk.

"Prepare to be boarded, captain."

Within minutes the cutter itself heaved into sight, moving fast, its sharp bow planing twin curls of foam off the sea. Soon a very rugged and expensive hard bottom inflatable sped towards us, and stopped a few yards off our beam. Four heavily armed men stared across the water.

"Is everyone on deck?" shouted the lieutenant.

"Unless we have a stowaway."

Their boat came alongside and gripping the main shrouds they nimbly slung themselves aboard. Our family faced a SWAT team, bristling with guns. Seven-year-old Diego, jaw agape, clung to his mother.

"This is a routine safety check, captain. . . sorry about the guns, what with your family and all . . . but we never know what we're going to run into out here."

The lieutenant took a quick look below, checking fire extinguishers and life jackets and opening the forward locker. I pried up a floorboard saying,

"You'll probably want to check in here for dope too — ."

"Don't bother," he answered. "We're not here to tear up your home. Let me sit down and finish off this boarding report."

I made us coffee and we ended up talking about boats. On deck the men were playing with our dog and recounting sea stories to our sons while eating fresh-baked banana bread. The bandoleered, hard-faced hit men were actually all-American boys, who waved good-bye fondly as they sped off at the head of a lavish white wake.

"Some safety check," I mused.

"Did they think we were sinking?" asked Diego.

"No, they were just looking for drugs. Or guns."

"On our boat?"

"Yup. The lieutenant said they try to check everything going through the Windward Passage."

"A big waste of taxpayers' money to harass us out here in the middle of nowhere," opined my wife.

"I suppose...I wonder what they really find."

"It was cool! I hope the jet buzzes us again." Diego had lost his apprehension.

We were bound for Great Inagua, just under the horizon, 40 miles north. With luck we would be there before midnight, off the soft lights of the town, riding at anchor in three fathoms of translucent water over a rippled sandy bottom that was clearly visible by full moonlight.

I anticipated an easy sail but instead the evening brought a fast moving cold front with squalls and a NW gale of wind in our teeth. I cursed our luck. Even if we could get to Matthewtown, Inagua's only settlement, its anchorage would be hopelessly exposed to the northwester. The only safe harbor that didn't require a brutal beat against the wind was fifty miles away, on an unlit lee shore in Haiti.... not a good option. So we double-reefed the main, changed down to the storm jib, and put the boat's head to the wind.

What a night! The crew hung on while the boat bucked and slammed over wall after wall of water, exploding luminous foam from her bow. Taut as a tuning fork, her rig hummed she lifted from every sea with scuppers full and streaming. Spray swept her decks like a flail. It was a glorious night, elemental and wild, but also utterly miserable for the watch who turned their backs to the weather like cattle caught in a blizzard.

We felt Inagua before we saw it. The wind veered north in the night and by dawn came off the island, giving us a welcome lee. The sun revealed a line of gray smudge on the horizon that slowly lengthened into a long featureless coast of dull green scrub. Then bright beach began to flash into view; then the iridescent leap of aquamarine shallows; and finally a long ribbon of white surf breaking on a fringing reef. We stood in for the shore and only tacked when the indigo of oceanic depths changed abruptly to soundings, where primeval Inagua towers up from the ocean floor a mile below and barely breaks the surface. We sailed along this awesome drop-off, so sheer that we could see golden coral heads and thickets of elk horn ascending the incline to our starboard, while to port we looked down the wavery shafts of sunlight descending into the beckoning abyss.

We finally dropped anchor in Molasses Bay, an untenable anchorage in the normal easterly winds; but with the norther blowing the bay was flat calm. Coral gardens and aisles of pure white sand were clearly laid out twenty feet beneath the shimmering surface. That evening we ate lobster for supper, which we snared out of coral heads near the boat.

The next morning a track ashore led me past pink saltpans and vibrant desert scrub to Matthewtown. The customs house was perched on a low cliff over the sea. The customs officer sat, his head in his hands, far away. He looked up with a start when I coughed.

"What do you want?" he asked warily.

"Me?...I came to clear customs."

"You...came to clear customs, eh?" he mimicked. "Then where is your boat? I don't see it out here." He gestured out the window at the roadstead where big swells, driven by the northwest wind and steepened by the three fathom shelf, crashed against the cliffs below us.

"I left it anchored at Molasses Bay, sir."

"Molasses Bay? What are you up to?" He glared. I kept quiet.

"Don't you know its illegal to anchor there before making your entry? You'll have to move it here immediately."

"With due respect sir, no way."

"What? Are you trying to defy the law of the Bahamas?"

"No sir...look at those rollers. The anchorage is dangerous."

"Then bring it into the boat harbor." The boat harbor was a teacup dynamited out of the coral rock, with a hair-raising entrance. With these seas running it was Russian roulette to try to get in.

"If you insist, sir...but I don't have any insurance and I'm unfamiliar with the harbor. Therefore perhaps you would pilot the boat in."

"I'm not a pilot."

"That's all right — so long as you accept responsibility to be sued in case of damages."

The man in the starched white uniform and pencil mustache shook his head dubiously, but finally nodded. I thought I detected the glimmer of a smile.

"Well, conditions are bad...OK, bring your boat over here tomorrow and anchor where I can see it from this window. Is that clear?"

The street outside was almost deserted except for some men clustered around the town's only public phone. Unshaven and disheveled, they looked like they'd spent the night on the floor in their clothes. They were Latin, not Bahamian, and their spokesman was pouring fervent bursts of Spanish into the phone. I asked the elderly clerk in a grocery store across the street who they were.

"Oh, you ain't hear?" His face lit up. "Dem is Colombian fellas. Dey boat get wreck in de storm night before las'. Dey be callin' all de day long to Barranquila for dey ticket home. Else dey be goin' jail."

"Why?"

"Boat loaded wi' ganja, mon. Plenty plenty ganja. Dey bring it here, transfer to a yacht at night. Den de norther come wreck de two a dem. All de ganja float out an' wash up on de beach — two t'ousan' poun'. You see de people dem? Dey lookin' seaweed!" He chortled, pointing at the shore where small knots of people, including old ladies and children, combed the flotsam.

Down the coast, just past the last houses, a fifty-foot fiberglass ketch lay impaled on rocks at the high tide line, masts canted at the sky. And in a rocky cove beneath the customs building I saw all that was left of the Colombian fishing boat — a mass of plywood fragments. The surf had demolished it, all except for a huge unpainted fiberglass fuel tank wedged between two rocks. It must have held a thousand gallons.

I was walking back when a brand new Toyota station wagon with 4-wheel drive, tinted glass and A/C offered me a ride. Inside sat three dapper young Inaguans, wearing Vuarnet shades, Gucci shoes and gold chains heavy enough to anchor a skiff. The driver wasted no time in fishing a spliff out of his pocket. A gold Rolex gleamed handsomely at his wrist as he lit the joint with a gold Zippo, puffed at it til the tip threw off sparks, then inhaled a prodigious cloud of pungent smoke.

"Want some?" he croaked, offering me the burning brand, as thick fumes wreathed his face and curled through his dread-locks.

"I think I got plenty just breathing."

"Good ganja mon."

"I don't doubt it. Is this the stuff from the boat that wrecked?"

"No, mon." He sounded aggrieved. "Dis ain' no sea-weed...dis quality smoke... Sensi! In Inagua we only smoke the best." At this we crested a low ridge and saw my boat riding at anchor.

"Nice vessel, mon. Where you buy she?"

"I built her myself."

"What is dis...! You's a hardworkin' man, for true. She could hold a lot a cargo?"

"Well...I once took six tons of French wine from St. Barths to St. John."

"Smugglin'?"

"Oh no... Not worth it."

"Right, right," he said quickly. "Got to worth it. Ain' no money in wine no how. But..." he shot me a significant look, "Ganja now, there's money. Imagine six tons of ganja!"

"Never fit on the boat. Wine is heavy. Ganja must be like hay."

"True, but five hundred pound now...you could hide that easy. Pick it up here, drap it Florida, all people you could trus'...good money, mon. Easy money." He looked very sincere. I said nothing and he was encouraged to continue. "We got plenty good ganja on Inagua, you know. Not to boast but we is big time here, we got the good location. Colombian fellas bring it to we, Yankee come and take it away. I build my mama a nice house las' year."

"Sounds kind of dangerous to me. What if that customs officer in Matthewtown catches you?" Whoops of laughter greeted this remark. "He? Oh Gaahd!" Tears of delight. "If only you know...he de las' mon to stop it!"

A couple of days later when it calmed down again we brought the boat around to the boat basin on the north edge of town. At a grocery store the proprietor beckoned me into an alcove surrounded by dusty cans of corned beef and offered to sell us grass. And the same day our cab driver looked stagily around to demonstrate that we were alone, then he too popped the question.

"Want to take some sensi to Florida? I can sell you a hundred pounds, cheap, cheap."

"Sorry, I don't invest money in dope."

"That's all right, I trust you. Just pay me when you get it sell."

"Is this the grass from the wrecked boat?"

He nodded.

"I thought the police burned it all."

"They burn some."

Years passed before we visited Inagua again. At first glance the anchorage and the sleepy town seemed unchanged — until we heard a thunderous roar in the west, and saw a huge military cargo plane coming in for a landing that shook the earth. The little dirt airstrip where they used to chase goats off before a flight had metamorphosed into a long tarmac runway. Aircraft with US Navy and Coast Guard markings sat parked at the side. There was a hangar, a row of prefab barracks, and from one of the roofs sprouted an impressive array of electronic dishes and antennae. Forklifts revved their motors, belching puffs of smoke, emitting beep-beeps as they backed up, unloading the plane.

As it turned out, Great Inagua's location, perfect for smugglers, was also perfect for a DEA/Coast Guard surveillance base to catch smugglers. The island's days as a free and easy backwater were numbered. But the Inaguans didn't seem to mind. There were a couple of new bars and restaurants, a new guesthouse, and steady taxi business between the base and town. The dust was gone from the shelves in the grocery stores.

For five centuries the island had seen a succession of livelihoods come and go, driven by events in the outside world. Wrecking, slaving, blockade-running, rum-running, salt farming, dope smuggling.... they'd all flourished in their hour. Now a new dispensation had arrived, and once again Great Inagua was tacking with the times, trimming its sails to the prevailing wind.

27.

FRENCH

Good news for gringos sailing south — in Venezuela we aren't the "ugly Americans" any more. Along the coast and in the islands we've been replaced as least favored nation by the French — who have developed a reputation there as arrogant moochers, if not arrant thieves.

I found that out when I tied up my dinghy at the yacht club in Puerto La Cruz, to buy ice. Immediately a uniformed worker with greasy hands came running from under a boat and gestured imperiously for me to stop. Offended by this pretentious flunky I walked on but at the office the manager started in on me — in Spanish, and none too friendly. Where was I going? What was I doing here? The premises were strictly forbidden to non-members.

Mystified, pissed, I muttered audibly, in English, "What the hell is going on here?"

"Oh...are you an American?" asked the boss, much taken aback.

"Yes...is that a problem?" I answered truculently.

"Please forgive me...I thought you were French! I mean, not that you look..." he trailed off; embarrassed, but eager to make amends. He spoke fluent English and had been educated in the States. He got out the ice himself while explaining that so many French yachtsmen had stolen things from the premises

— fenders, line, tools, fuel cans, even outboards — that they were banned from the yacht club unless they were staying at a slip...and paid up in advance. "But Americans" — he beamed — "no problem!"

One gets used to British sailors having an attitude about "the Frogs" out of jealousy over their wine and women, but an anti-French attitude in South Americans came as a surprise. Nevertheless we found it repeated place after place. At Carenero the French were unwelcome, in fact for a time even forbidden. Mention the Gauls at the Macuto Sheraton and you got a suspicious frown. And it had been French sailors who so abused the hospitality of the Puerto Azul yacht club that anchorage was now off limits to all yachts. This was a major blow to yachts transiting that stretch of the coast, but the club had its provocations. In fact, I had been there for the incident that had precipitated the ban.

Puerto Azul is Venezuela's biggest country and yacht club. It nestles at the base of towering, jungled mountains where the Naiguata river has cut a gorge in the coastal range and deposited enough sediment into the sea to give a boat's anchor good holding on a narrow shelf of sand. Here the club built a long high breakwater that provided the only shelter in sixty miles of bold coast.

Naturally it was a popular stop for sailors working east or west, especially since the marina allowed access to the highway outside the premises where buses could be caught to La Guaira and Caracas.

The marina bar and restaurant were open to visiting sailors but the rest of the club's facilities were specifically off limits. A group of French yachties in the harbor was nevertheless in the habit of attending the free movies and using the pool. No one minded, they told me, and those who did were bourgeois prigs. They persuaded me, against my better judgment, to attend a movie with them. But when we got there — my French friends unshaven, dressed in tattered shorts and their girlfriends' nipples straining against their filmy blouses — I could see unmistakable disapproval on the conservative club members' faces.

We got so many hostile looks I left partly through the movie, uncomfortable with the vibes.

Apparently, that was the straw that broke the camel's back. Next morning a launch made the rounds of the harbor, distributing flyers to every boat informing them that non-members were no longer permitted to anchor within the yacht club breakwater. That hurt the whole yachting fraternity.

Yet another French-provoked incident threatened the important breakwater harbor at Caraballeda — the best free anchorage near Caracas. As I was walking up the steps from the river to the Capitania de Puerto, I heard heated voices coming from the Capitania. A bearded Frenchman stalked out, wearing khaki shorts, with muscular hairy legs like a French colonial policeman. He was ushered out by a fuming official. Curtly he asked for my papers and I feared that my welcome had been jeopardized — but when he looked at my passport a smile warmed up his face. "Ah...American..." He relaxed a little.

Then he told me that the Frenchman had anchored inside the main harbor breakwater. Quite a few boats were anchored stern-to there, in an area traditionally fished by small boats. One of them had got his hook tangled in the Frenchman's anchor chain — which stretched halfway across the harbor — and as they tried to free it the fellow had aimed a rifle at their heads and ordered them off immediately.

The port captain searched the boat in vain for the gun. The Frenchman accused the teenagers of being potential thieves, and spoke his mind about Venezuela and Venezuelans. Retelling the incident, this port captain snorted indignantly. If he had to choose between foreign yachts trying to moor for free or his own countrymen trying to eat....!

Everywhere up and down the coast it was the same complaint.... French were even accused of stealing the solar panels that powered lights marking dangerous reefs and cays.

This amazed us. These days we assume that prejudice is a black-white problem, but evidently it can be found anywhere — in this variant, in this corner of the world, it is the French as dirty, thieving and arrogant "frogs." My own stereotypes ran along the lines of the Marquis de Lafayette and Brigitte Bardot...pretty favorable. We had met some French sailors in the Med and liked them. So what was going on here?

Sailing is a national passion in France. The largest yacht-building company in the world is Beneteau. Some of the most famous sailors in the world are French, notably the late Bernard Moitessier who exhibited the incomparable cool, when he was weeks ahead in the homestretch of the first single-handed round-the-world race, of passing up the last easy leg to the finish line near England in favor of continuing at sea to his home in the South Pacific. He fired the national imagination with his sea worthy, no-frills boat and simple, even austere lifestyle — poor in money, rich in experience.

His example sent out waves of young French sailors, audacious and poor, who left France in flotillas of cheap steel hulls, with next to no equipment, afire to see the world, to just do it, and ASAP too, no plodding along til every last bit of safety equipment was bought and installed, but leave — now — and outfit their vessels underway with whatever they could beg, borrow or steal. Hence, if you were tied up to a French vessel at a dock you were well advised to count your fenders as it left.

One had to admire the way they sailed everywhere in their ubiquitous, hard-chine steel hulls. French boats were predominant in the forbidding but spectacular Straits of Magellan. They hung out in Salvador de Bahia and Cap Haitien, dicey third world ports where most Americans or British would feel decidedly uncomfortable. While most Anglophone yachts heading across the Atlantic gave Africa a wide berth, the French stopped for months in Senegal's Casamance River.

But, the French sailors stuck to themselves, having a traditional dislike of speaking English which, in the age of English as the undisputed international language, seems cliquish and petty — to English speakers. And they were perceived as feeling somewhat cooler than the rest of us

What irks us isn't so much the assumption of superiority, which is common to every culture, but the backing for the claim. I mean, who cares if some Stone Age jungle tribe con-

siders themselves the apex of humanity. They may not even survive as a culture; their belief is quaint — not threatening. But
the Jews now — the people that produced Jesus, Bob Dylan
and Einstein — they have a plausible case for considering themselves God's Chosen; likewise the Japanese, or the
Germans...from such high-powered peoples, it rankles. As it
does from the French.

The French had made an art form out of arrogance. I'll
never forget the haughty-looking Parisian yuppie eating a loaf
of crumbly French bread at Le Select, in St. Barths. The bartender with difficulty held his tongue, watching the guy as he
shredded bread all over the counter, making a mess without
the slightest concern. Finally the bartender confronted the fellow and gestured at the crumbs all over the counter. The Parisian
considered for a moment — and then meticulously brushed
the crumbs off the counter, onto the bartender's feet.
Breathtakingly arrogant. Even the bartender was impressed and
just threw up his hands and walked off.

So anyway, hanging around English sailors I picked up a little anti-French bias myself, if only just to fit in — I didn't sub-
scribe to it the way the Brits did. And if I ever did, that was
put to rest permanently one stormy morning at Governor's
Harbor in Eleuthera in the Bahamas.

The engine had seized up a week previously and we were
sailing for Nassau to get it fixed. We ghosted in to Governor's
Harbour under full sail in the late afternoon sunshine of a very
clear day. A whaler marked Club Med came whizzing by with
two men in it. They did an admiring slow circle around us and
raised thumbs up. The boat did look good. She was on her
maiden voyage, her solid spars gleamed with virgin varnish, her
sails from flying jib to gaff mizzen were still snow white.

Governor's Harbour I'd read about for years in West Indian
history books as the chief town of the Eleutheran Adventurers
who first settled the Bahamas back in the 1500's. This had been
an important harbor for 400 years. It lay in an arm of land that
hooked over and around the harbor, leaving it exposed only to
the northwest. Houses were built up the sides of the harbor as

in Gustavia — stone lower walls, wooden uppers with painted fretwork on the verandahs. It looked a good anchorage for the night. The clear water showed a rippled, clean sand bottom for the anchor to get a deep grip.

After dropping the hook I'd gone ashore to have a couple of beers and found myself talking to the locals in a small bar. They were badmouthing the new Club Med, recently built on the beach next to town, and I dutifully weighed in with an anecdote about the French penchant for public nudity that goes way beyond topless beaches.

There is a spectacular anchorage in St. Lucia where the bottom falls away so steeply that yachts have to anchor stern to the shore, side by side with other boats. I came on deck early in the morning to enjoy the coolness of the air and the scent of frangipani wafting from the slopes. Sipping black coffee and taking deep contented breaths, I felt quietly exalted by the close presence of the mountains that rise like pillars out of the translucent depths. Just then, up from the cabin of the neighboring French boat emerged a bloat-bellied lout with bloodshot eyes and a stumbling gait. Wincing at the light, he dropped his drawers close enough for me to see inflamed pimples on pallid buttocks. I fled below, my morning reverie shattered.

I thought to myself at the time that it was a little shameful to repeat this story — but I did, wanting to have something to add to the conversation. Then I went home.

Next morning we awoke to rain and rising wind. Tropical storm Barry had suddenly and quite unexpectedly formed overnight from a mere easterly wave and was passing close by, its squalls blowing more and more from the unprotected NW quadrant of the harbor. Worse, we were dragging, slowly but steadily towards the shore where big waves crashed against the beach. Our engine was out, and the dinghy deflated on deck in preparation for an early departure.

I shoved the 70-lb. Bruce anchor over the side, paid out line and waited for it to fetch up. It dragged too, in nice tandem with my trusty 75-lb. CQR on ½-inch chain.

I discovered that the clean-rippled sand that looked like

such good holding was actually only a thin layer over a bed of loose coral. A fisherman anchor with its long pointed fluke was called for but the breakers were too close to allow me to drop it off the bow and pay out sufficient scope. I started frantically pumping up my dinghy in order to take the fisherman out to windward, but things looked bad. It wouldn't be easy to row against the strong wind, and we were quickly dragging into shallow water.

Just then at the Club Med two daring guys launched a skiff from the beach, skillfully timing the heavy surf, even so coming within an ace of capsizing before the motor fired up and shot them over the wave tops with audible thumps. They came up alongside our bow, seeing my plan at a glance. I lowered the fisherman into their skiff, a ticklish maneuver in five-foot seas with my bowsprit heaving up and down while the skiff ricocheted madly and threatened to swamp. Fearlessly these guys grabbed the anchor and took the anchor chain and then my bobstay came down hard on the one guy's head. Blood and rain streamed down his face and blew off his chin. I shouted, "My God, are you all right?" He shouted back, "Zis?" he gestured scornfully at his cut — "gif more chain!" They drove my anchor out 250 feet to the end of its scope and dropped it, then sprang aboard and helped me winch the boat to safety.

Those guys saved my boat. They were the same two who'd circled it the day before, admiring the gaff rig. Later, when I thought of the cheap jokes I'd made about "frogs" in the bar the previous night I was truly ashamed. To this day I can't forget the French guy, in the rain and heaving seas, rivulets of blood streaming down his face: "Gif more chain!"

What can you say about the nation that gave us champagne and the bikini? So…they may have a few light-fingered bad apples — what nation doesn't? And maybe one of them even did steal the solar panels from the light on the Las Aves Reef — if so may he wreck his boat on that very reef and drown. But to the great majority of his countrymen, who keep their pants on in public and only take what's theirs I still say "Vive La France!"

28.

LIGNUM VITAE

There's a fine line between passion and obsession and I think I may have just crossed it the day I staggered home with my big score. At least that's what my wife said when she saw the blood.

"Obsession?" I remonstrated. "That's about money, nymphets or drugs — you know, vice." Still, I know what she means. It is a bit unusual to go to such efforts for a piece of wood... yet...yet...for an astonishing wood. If I'm obsessed over anything it's how something like a lignum vitae tree can spring from a half-inch seed. It reminds me of the Big Bang.

The first piece of lignum vitae I ever saw was on a boat in Gustavia's inner harbor many years ago. St. Barths was still relatively undiscovered then, except by sailors, who liked the quaint teacup harbor surrounded by hills, and the island's genial laissez-faire. The old town dock always had a rakish West Indian schooner taking on cases of duty-free scotch to smuggle into the islands south of there. It was also a freewheeling locus of pot smuggling under sail. Marijuana smugglers came and went, shedding money at fine restaurants like a wet dog shaking off water.

Some memorable characters could be found hanging out in

that harbor, carousing at Le Select, the inspiration of Jimmy Buffet's "Cheeseburger in Paradise." Prime among them was Paul Johnson, a legendary voyager whose weathered features, wild hair and booming laughter created a center of attention wherever he went. Master mariner, artist and womanizer, not to mention a rum drinker, noted boat builder and raconteur, Paul had more deep sea miles under his keel than anybody I knew. He was no smuggler; to the contrary he was fond of boasting, in front of rich scammers who were smug about their new wealth, that he lived happily on $200 a month, and enjoyed a life far beyond his means. Coming from the saltiest voyager of them all, it tended to dampen the talk about Swiss banks and favorite champagnes.

We were aboard his boat one day, drinking lukewarm tank water made palatable by the addition of rum and lime—ice being a luxury he generally did without — when he slid across the table, with a significant look, the carving of a dolphin. At once I was taken by the wood — stripes of light yellow and dark brown that had been polished to a rare luster. The wood was incredibly hard, and heavy as any stone, yet warm and alive. It sat in my hand, smooth as silk, gleaming like a precious element.

"Is this wood?" I asked

"Is gold a metal?" he replied. "It's lignum vitae, the heaviest densest hardest wood in the world, and actually it's a damn sight more useful than gold. Look here..." he pulled up a floorboard and showed me a gray slab that I could scarcely lift.

"I keep it for spares — you can make anything out of it — from bushings to bullets...!"

"Where do you find it?" I asked.

"It's hard to come by...but I'll cut you off a piece. Any more you'll have to find on your own."

I took my piece back to my boat and carved a round, polished handle for an ice pick whose handle had splintered. Now, instead of just an ice pick it became a marine surveyor's tool, the handle a perfect tapping hammer and the pick a probe.

As I cut and shaped the wood I felt a mild euphoria. Working it made me feel good, and others have noted this as well. At the time I attributed it to the beauty of the wood, and to the subtle smell, vaguely reminiscent of chocolate. Now I wonder if freshly cut lignum vitae might be slightly psychoactive, perhaps some molecule in its complex, little-understood resin stimulates endorphins. I wanted more....but like they say about real estate, they aren't making any more of it.

Lignum vitae once grew profusely in the West Indies but became increasingly rare in the 20th century. One of the longest lived of trees, it is also one of the slowest growing, and when fully grown attains only 15 to 30 feet in height. The supply was plentiful as long as the demand was just Indians making their war swords and clubs of lignum vitae, but once the Europeans latched onto it...

Many a corsair who sailed to the West Indies dreaming of sacking a city or seizing the treasure fleet ended up filling his hold with lignum vitae — not a golden fortune but a profitable cargo to sell to Europe's shipwrights and apothecaries. It had a wide range of uses aboard ship. Its hardness and oiliness was ideal for making blocks (pulleys), of which every ship used hundreds. The chronometers used in shipboard navigation had lignum vitae clockwork mechanisms that were self-lubricating and wouldn't expand or contract despite extremes in temperature. Extract of the wood and its remarkable resin was prescribed to cure the "French Pox", as the English snidely referred to syphilis. Even today old West Indian fishermen swear by lignum vitae tea as a treatment for fish poisoning.

When the steam ship arrived on the scene lignum vitae's self-lubricating qualities made it the universal choice for propeller shaft bearings, until modern ships became too numerous and too large — an aircraft carrier spins a propeller shaft 11 feet in diameter. Ashore the wood was made into everything from dentures (George Washington had some lignum vitae teeth), to bowling balls and became so scarce and valuable that today it is sold by weight — when available.

I learned something in the Exumas, anchored in the Pipe

Cays where channels of unbelievably radiant water lace together a network of cays. One day, while following turtle tracks in the sand — their flippers make marks like tractor tires — I came upon a lignum vitae foundation post still upright in the corner of a ruined house. I dug it out of the ground and gave it a whack with the machete to see how badly rotted it was underneath the layer of dirt — and the impact sent a jolt up my arm. It was like hitting concrete. The bright amber of fresh cut wood glowed. I learned later from a shopkeeper at Staniel Cay that house had stood for 75 years before blowing away in a hurricane back in the twenties. 150 years that post had been in the ground…!

That made me think — if lignum vitae was so durable then there should be lots of pieces left — if one knew where to look. Henceforward, when on hikes in the West Indies I kept a weather eye out for ruined houses, old fence posts, gnarled silvery stumps. From what I found I made things useful and pleasing to my life.

I carved jewelry for my wife, a highly polished pelican, with emerald eyes that hung from a fine gold chain. I made her chopping boards and cheese plates, serving spoons, a mortar and pestle, a garlic crusher. For my sons I carved a chess set. For my boat I fabricated handles, cleats, fairleads, sway hooks, deadeyes, pad eyes, belaying pins, and parrel beads. I used it, in a pinch, to shim up the gearbox mounts. Of course I had lignum vitae shaft bearings — and when the young daughter of my dear friends died, her hand-built coffin went to rest with her name engraved onto a lignum vitae heart affixed to the outside of the casket.

One day recently I was following an old fence line in one of the most rugged and remote parts of St. John when I came across a donkey trail which I took, only to end up in an extensive patch of "catch and keep" — a vicious bush whose innumerable tiny sharp cat's claws grip anything that blunders into it. The more one tries to disengage, the more entangled one gets. The only escape is to bolt out headlong, like tearing a bandaid off a hairy arm. I steeled myself, lunged forward and broke loose, suffering a score of cuts — and tripped over a fallen limb. I turned to curse it, but held my tongue. I had stumbled over the biggest, most perfect log of lignum vitae that I had ever seen, just laying there, maybe for centuries.

My find absorbed me for several days. I returned with a five-foot timber saw, cut the 12-foot log into barely manageable lengths, slashed a rough trail and staggered up and down hill with each piece weighing nearly as much as a sack of cement. I got stung by jack Spaniards (local wasps whose black and yellow coloring matched the conquistadors' uniforms), I brushed my neck against poisonous Christmas bush, phalanxes of agave spears stabbed me time and again, a fearsome cassia thorn pierced my shoe sole and my foot as well — and I stressed my back for several months to come.

When my wife got back from a weeklong trip she found me unable to straighten my back, my arms badly scratched, my face swollen, limping on an infected foot.

"What on earth happened to you?" She asked, and when she heard, made the reference to "obsession."

I don't care...now I have a treasure trove stashed below my house. Just the thought of it warms my heart...

29.

ICE AGENTS AND BREAD BROKERS

After a rough crossing from Bequia, Breath motored up St. Vincent's smooth lee, nearing Wallilabou Bay, our destination for the night. We moved along steadily, about two miles offshore, just our boat and the magic mountain moving past, steep peaks shining and deep valleys enshadowed in the afternoon's slanting light. None of us noticed the skiff.

Then we heard a shout and spotted a sleek little double-ended whaleboat being rowed towards us at breakneck speed by a young man with a head of springy dreadlocks. At every stroke of the oars the skiff surged forward, a flower of foam blossoming, then wilting, at its throat.

My son Raff eased the throttle into neutral. We drifted to a halt.

"What's the problem?" Raff bellowed across the water.

"Me name Liston Joseph but dey calls me 'Roots Man.' I gon' get you banana, grapefruit, mango, avocado — anyt'ing you want jus' aks for Roots Man. I talk wi' you first — right?"

He held up his painter, mutely suggesting a tow, but we declined, feeling a bit put off. We had expected to render assistance, not to find ourselves trifled with; so we proceeded, while he, not the least rebuffed, followed in our wake.

Well. We apparently had just met the advance guard of the controversial Wallilabou boat boys cartel about whom we'd heard much — mostly negative — from cruising sailors. The captain of an English motor sailor, who had been fulminating in a bar in Admiralty Bay, after downing several stiff Mount Gays, expressed the gist of it.

"They're incredibly aggressive — they accost you before you get the hook down, shouting and milling about while you're trying to position the anchor. Cheeky buggers wouldn't take no for an answer — damn near had to run 'em off with a shotgun. Bloody nuisance, I say. Wouldn't go back there again — they've ruined the place!"

Rounding the next bluff we opened up the notorious Wallilabou Bay and, sure enough, our arrival set off the nautical equivalent of the Oklahoma land stampede, as water craft put helter-skelter out to sea like salvagers racing for a rich wreck. A youth lying on a wind surfer board and stroking hand over hand led the way, hotly pursued by a dinghy rowed so hard it leaped in staccato, and by a lad valiantly sculling a mutilated Boston Whaler, showing foam core and mangled glass where its bow once had been. Right where we wanted to anchor, two fellows paddled about restively in truck tire inner tubes. Swimmers brought up the rear guard.

Like many anchorages in the Windwards, the bottom at Wallilabou drops off so rapidly that a boat needs to anchor and then take a stern line ashore to prevent the anchor dragging off into deep water.

By the time we got ready to perform this maneuver they had clustered round so tightly we feared hitting one of them. They clung to the side of our boat, to the bobstay beneath our anchors, clamoring to take a line ashore or to sell us bananas. Not wanting to catch a loose line or limb in the prop I asked them to clear away from the stern but nobody listened to a word, so intent were they on out-maneuvering each other. Having overshot my spot and drifted too close to another boat, I roared out, "Stay clear of the ___ prop!" and revved it in reverse. They gave way momentarily, dodged the anchor as it dropped, and closed in again.

Just then up rowed Roots Man, all sweaty and panting,

heatedly proclaiming his rights. By comparison with the others he looked pretty good now, clearly possessed of the best claim, not to mention the best boat; and so we gave him the nod — and with that the hubbub ceased. We had made our choice. The rag tag fleet dispersed, laughing and bantering as they returned to their stakeout points. Even now the next yacht approached.

Roots Man took our line ashore and tied it expertly to a steel stake, then returned to take our order for fresh fruit — and anything else we might need. He had contacts for everything. His mother baked us bread and made ice in five-gallon buckets kept for a day in her rust-riddled freezer; an uncle's farm supplied limes, grapefruit, papaya, bananas and fresh nutmeg; his sisters did our laundry in a stream, beating our clothes against a smooth rock and hanging them out to dry on a thorn bush.

There were other benefits too, not the least of which was the easy shunting off of would-be guides — we already belonged to Roots Man. When we walked ashore he and his buddies kept an eye on our boat. His pride was now involved; anybody who stole from us was disrespecting him and his livelihood.

This connection cost us little because we needed to buy fruits and vegetables anyway — we deliberately omitted them from our shopping earlier, figuring we might as well go through one of the boat boys in Wallilabou. We'd have to deal with them one way or another, and once on good terms with a boat-boy you get more than your purchases — you get local knowledge, a guard, perhaps even the makings of a friend.

The Wallilabou boat boy cartel is the latest wrinkle on a syndrome that is spreading in the Caribbean and elsewhere as far-flung as Gambia, Turkey, and Brazil — wherever yachts congregate in poor countries. At its crux is the explosion in the number of cruising yachts in recent decades and their tendency to cluster in certain popular anchorages. Simultaneously TV, radio and movies have raised the awareness, if not the income, of Third World people — many of whom feel that if you can afford to come to their country to enjoy it you can afford to employ the inhabitants now and then. Where the occasional passing yacht used to be a novelty, and its crew was treated like guests, now that they have become a constant presence, an institution, they are increasingly seen as customers, if not marks.

Venezuela is a case in point. We first cruised there in 1974, shortly after the coast became safe to visit, as their guerrilla threat had faded away. Previously, the Venezuelan navy had taken a dim view of foreign yachts, seeing them as potential arms smugglers and mistakenly shot up enough to effectively discourage casual cruisers. When we came through we were the first yacht in many anchorages that people had seen in years and they treated us as valued guests. People went out of their way to see that we had a good time.

At the entrance to Mochima, a fjord-like five-mile long indentation on Venezuela's Caribbean coast, we unwittingly anchored in the middle of their seine net fishing area. The fishermen insisted that we stay put, dragged their nets all around us, and even roared by just after dawn to throw three snappers, cleaned and incised for garlic, into our cockpit. But subsequently, Mochima became a very popular yachting rendezvous and when we returned some years later to the same spot a fishing boat immediately sped out to us and with scowls forbid us to anchor anywhere near the village.

Puerto La Cruz had changed too. A host of yachts were anchored off the town where a handful had been, and when we beached the dinghy we were met by the dinghy guardians who for a reasonable fee would ensure that when you wished to return to your yacht you would still have oars and outboard and intact conveyance in which to do so. Having heard about the recent rash of dinghy robberies along the coast we were glad to pay.

Being confronted by a crowd of people demanding employment, or exorbitant fees, or protection money goes against anybody's grain. Sailors can be especially annoyed by the assorted bread brokers, fruit factors and ice agents because we pride ourselves on being self-sufficient. We certainly don't want a guide to buy fruits and vegetables, since one of the best ways to meet the people and pick up a few rudiments of the language is to shop daily for fresh produce. After all, we're not staying in some fancy hotel buffered from reality by air conditioning and tinted glass. We didn't fly here on a jet at 28,000 feet. If we can get here on our own steam we can get around on our own as well.

That's why there is such a testy response to the boat boys, guides and professional "friends" who want to do for money what we prefer to do for ourselves. They encroach on the core value of cruising — self sufficiency; and they infringe on a precious Anglo-Saxon right, that cornerstone of modern American culture — the right to privacy. If a boat is one's castle, the abrasive boatboys are Goths beating at its walls. The natural reaction is to defend one's wallet and privacy by stonewalling, temporizing — to send them packing, ideally. It took an episode in Haiti to show me the flip side.

Everything is exaggerated, more extreme in Haiti and this was especially true of its guides. A gang of them lay in wait at the head of the main shipping dock in Port-au-Prince, where we were moored for six weeks. They clenched the bars of the gate, and were held back only by the bored, sullen "ton ton macoute" patrolling with a pistol stuck in his waist, a casual place to carry a piece to commit a casual murder.

Once through the gate you were fair game and had to run a gauntlet of aggressive guides who were in your face, begging, cajoling, threatening, and waving tattered documents. It became apparent that to get any peace we would have to choose one...if only for him to run off the others. It gave a new twist to the expression "forced labor" — they forced their labor on you. Qualified mainly by a smattering of English and bulldog persistence, they had seen an abrupt falling off in their business since the AIDS stigma scared off the cruise ships. Competition was fierce. One of them would ingeniously manage to engage you in conversation while warding off the other guides with threats, pleas and jokes. Once he established his property rights with them, you were his. He'd won you fair and square.

"You American? Oh I love American. American love me, I

working two year on American yacht, I have letter, very honest worker...Texas? You know Texas?...How 'bout New York? You wan' buy mango, go Iron Market? Right, right, I show you, get you good price!"

Having been through this the day before, you might insist that you didn't need a guide, wished to be left alone, knew your way and would not pay a cent. No matter; he would hang along at a slight remove and keep up a running commentary meant to be informative, hail vendors imperiously, bargain for you, and suggest short cuts. If once you followed a suggestion no matter whether it was already your intention anyway, it was a done deal. You had an employee to whom you owed wages. Actually refusing to pay him could create a vehement scene, with waved fists and threats to get a gun.

I finally won a round though. My wife and I went out the gates one night when there were fewer guides and one of them took up station and began his rap in English. Resigned, we ignored him and kept walking. Thinking we might be European, he switched into fluent French, and after awhile, equally fluent Spanish. I was impressed. A kid in his twenties in command of three foreign languages. We kept silent and listened to him try a succession of tongues whose rudiments he'd picked up from ships calling at the dock, Italian, German, Tagalog ...what was perhaps Urdu — and a smattering of Greek he'd been learning from the freighter next to us that had been waiting two weeks for cargo.

This earnest young man was an impressive, self-taught linguist — but I suddenly had an idea I couldn't resist. Ever since living in Hong Kong as a boy I could mimic Chinese passably well so I turned and asked him as though I really needed to know something,

"Ching chow mein egg foo young Chou En Lai? Ho Chi Minh mai-tai Szechuan wun hun glo?"

It floored him. He stood there open mouthed but for once with nothing to say. Then he caught himself, politely waved good-bye and ran back to the dock. My big triumph in Haiti — and I was too ashamed to laugh.

He was revenged not long afterwards by the most remarkable beggar-cum-hustler I've ever confronted. It was at the Iron Market, the huge black iron framework in the heart of the city that houses such an eclectic display of everything produced in the country: sacks of corn, coffee and vanilla, dead pigs and live ducks, piles of every tropical fruit, seed and shell jewelry, spices and herbs of magic and aphrodisiac repute, hairy-legged swamp-crabs bound and squirming in a basket, and large frogs tethered by the waist, not to mention an endless display of paintings and carvings ranging from the crude to the sublime. My wife was bargaining for some grapefruits when a wary look crossed the vendor's face. A hand plucked at my sleeve.

I turned to see a middle-aged woman with a battered face and glittering eyes. Her torn blouse exposed flopping breasts and her long skirt bore testimony to a life in the gutter. She made the hungry sign, stuck out her hand, and rocked back on her heels, and gave a hideous bleat like a deranged goat.

I tried to move away, embarrassed, and repelled by the aggressive glint in her darting eyes, but a quick crowd had gathered tight around us to watch and I noticed contempt and anticipation in their faces. Now she fixed me with a glare, her eyes like Rasputin and then reached her free hand deliberately down to her crotch and grabbed...something...I don't know what it was! It must have been an 18-inch tumor protruding from her groin like a Dak salami.

She unquestionably had my attention now.

With a malevolent grin, she squeezed it hard, and started slapping it against her thigh and bleated like an orgasmic sheep, all the while demanding money with a grasping claw.

I'm not ashamed to admit that I stood mesmerized, a rodent before a snake. I fumbled automatically for money and gave her I don't know how much, but it satisfied her and she stopped and walked off with a triumphant smirk. I was left wondering if she was for real, or if I had been masterfully conned. Given the state of reality in Haiti she could have been a pathetically deformed mute maddened by suffering, or a woman of brilliant insight who recognized an opportunity and grabbed it by the throat. If so she must have made a small fortune in the days when cruise ships dropped thousands of Middle American matrons at the Iron Market to shop for souvenirs. My guess is that she had a stuffed snake strapped to her thigh, but I didn't have the wits or the guts to ask to see it.

The incident with that woman left me stunned but the incident with the young linguist made me reconsider these "people at the gate." Here was a gifted individual eager to work at the best outlet available given the chronic lack of opportunity that was Haiti.

Maybe the Goths beating on the castle walls were just pleading for shelter from the storm, desperately hoping to be noticed. Maybe the aggressive posture is merely a matter of necessity, — not an inherent, obnoxious personal trait. It's a function of the high unemployment rate — with so many people desperate for work and no organized system to apportion the limited opportunities, one has to be aggressive, insistent and "in your face" just to be heard.

Furthermore, just because someone's reason for "being your friend" transparently involves a one way flow of money — your money — doesn't necessarily preclude an interesting relationship or even a friendship of sorts. To write someone off because he wanted money was naive. Everybody's got to eat. If you're going to travel in the third world, you might as well get used to it — money is always involved in friendship, at some level, though it may not be immediately obvious.

For instance, we hired Roots Man to guide us on a long hike to a spectacular waterfall that we could never have found on our own. Twenty years ago I would have waited til I made an acquaintance or friend, who would have guided me there for the pleasure of my company, thereby assuring myself of an authentic experience. However — he would have ended up asking for a gift anyway, or if not I would have felt obliged to help him out with some pressing financial need — school fees for his child, medicine for his wife — he's a friend after all, and what price does one put on a friendship? It was cheaper, not to mention less complicated, to pay Roots Man.

Not only did we get a tour of the lush countryside, we got an entree into the milieu of his peers "the real Rastas," practicing Rastafarians who eat no meat, work the land, shun Babylon (urban life and material culture) and devote themselves to their families, to Jah, and to ganja — marijuana. As Roots Man's entourage we enjoyed a warm reception and cool lemon grass tea. Behind the Medusa-like dreadlocks and reddened eyes we got to know some likable and extremely colorful characters. With their rough garb smelling of wood smoke, their beards and hair uncut, carrying shepherds' crook staffs, and intoning cryptic scriptural aphorisms, they resembled a convocation of Old Testament prophets — Jeremiah, Samuel and Isaiah — high on ganja.

So now, instead of seeing third world employment-seekers as opponents to be stonewalled or outwitted, I consider them one way, an easy way, to get to know a native of the country who speaks English — a human resource one can use to mutual advantage. Why not employ a likely lad at an agreed upon pittance to fetch the diesel or the beer, to lead you to the right buses for a ride through the environs, or procure for you the fresh produce, ice or bread you're going to buy anyway. Spread the money out to the small guys instead of funneling it into a marina or supermarket.

It's a small, personal way to participate in the development of the third world, to pick and choose a worthy recipient of your foreign aid dollar rather than have it wind up in the sticky fingers of a government that will steal or waste it or use it to buy arms. On a one-to-one level you have a much better chance of making good choices than some bureaucrat in Washington even if your shrewdness as a judge of character is limited.

And if you're traveling by yacht, you'll find that the boat-boys at least will stop pestering you because they recognize you've paid your dues. Besides, they are busy — prospecting for that mother lode — that mythical American who pays everyone according to New York City union wages.

30.

BEAT THE BANK

The afternoon sun burned our backs as we clung to the top of the barge's ramp and squinted fervently into the distance. We weren't looking for land — land encompassed us, though we couldn't see any of it. Instead we were looking for water, specifically, deep enough water to get us outa here!

Instead, a vast maze of grassy shallows laced here and there by channels of deeper water stretched away to the horizon. All about us the water was scarcely a foot or two deep — and getting less as the tide dropped. For hours we had followed one channel after another, picking a new one up as an old one gave out — but this time we had followed a channel too far, powering on and on as the sides — long lines of drying sandbars — grew closer together and the water under our flat bottom grew less, until we had to stop.

In the distance another channel beckoned. I watched a small flock of little wading birds arrive at the drying sandbar to our right and start patrolling the water's edge, darting their beaks into the wet sand. We might be neighbors soon…because we were stranded smack dab in the middle of the great Caicos Bank.

Ironically, it was a bank that got us into this fix in the first place. Breeze had gotten a bank loan in St. Thomas to buy the barge and was supposed to pick up the funds at the Jacksonville branch. However, interest rates back then had hit an historic high, around 20%, and the money, though it had been sent, just couldn't seem to arrive. It disappeared for two full weeks as every hand it passed through detained it for just a little while, avidly goosing it for interest. Meanwhile the five of us were crammed into one room at a Best Western, eating junk food at cheap chain restaurants, our lives on indefinite hold.

"Breeze" was the captain and owner, soon to be in the barge business back in the Virgin Islands — if we ever got there! The rest of us had come along to help, me as navigator, Calis as mechanic, Bucky and Leon as deck hands.

The day before the seller finally had to leave — with his barge — the money popped up. Things improved greatly once we cast off, in a hurry to make up for so much lost time. The two big diesels hammered away inside the bare steel hull sounding like chainsaws ripping into a tin roof.

We crossed the Gulf Stream, stopped in Nassau for fuel and filters and pushed on to Beacon Cay at the north end of the magical Exumas chain. We arrived in the late afternoon...and stopped to fish for our supper.

We shut off the deafening engines and sat listening to the sudden quiet which washed over our ears. Afternoon sunlight gilded the wet rocks and flashed on the gleaming bodies of the jumping fry like a shower of silver coins tossed in a pretty arc.

Out came the lines and reels — a scrap of chicken for bait — and a great satisfaction settled down over the barge, as the guys chatted for a bit, then fell silent and fished.

Calis and I put on snorkel gear and slipped into a sea of phenomenal visibility. It teemed with brilliant little fish. Lavender sea fans waved languidly back and forth, like metronomes keeping beat to the sea's pulse. Tube sponges of rich grey and blue stood out from the bottom Bonito flashed by fast and furious, zigzagging a hundred times a minute, while clusters and veils of tiny translucent silversides draped themselves around branches of elk horn coral. Then we saw a shark materialize out of the blue like a ghost coming through a wall.

© Don E. Brown 2004

Just before dark we ate fried fish and fungi, a West Indian favorite. Then we resumed our voyage, running all night down the deep and wide Exuma Sound.

Next day we picked up Rum Cay. Like most of the low lying Bahamas, Rum Cay was first discernible as a smudge on the horizon growing into a series of low humps that gradually connected into a long line of dull green scrub with a beach glinting beneath it.

We passed just a hundred yards off its westernmost point — a dazzling extrusion of bright white sand, shot through with pink and gold and heaped high by northerly swells. From beach down to the sea floor was a plunge through color, a flawless progression from palest green to deepest indigo.

We were tied to the dock at Mayaguana when the mail boat came in. More than mail it carried everything the islanders needed from Miami and Nassau. When it arrived, half the island showed up in Toyota pick-up trucks. Off came — more pick ups — plus appliances, mattresses, lumber, cement, roofing, food, packages of every size. People crowded the dock. The blur of activity only came to an end when everything was unloaded and the small ship left.

That night people came by to invite us to a fund-raising party at the schoolhouse where we made some friends, ate, drank, laughed and had a grand time. An old man told me an amazing story that the people standing around listening swore was true.

The man had been teen-aged boy with his father and uncle on a 25-foot fishing smack well out from land when the weather rapidly deteriorated. They headed back for shelter on Mayaguana but their sails blew out in the rising squalls and they were adrift when big seas started to break around them. One of them crashed onto the sloop and stove in the cabin side. The boat went down quickly and the boy found himself alone in tumultuous seas. A hatch cover gave him something to cling to and he rode it that day and night, gripping onto it for dear life. The storm passed by leaving calm fine weather in its wake. Another day and night went by. The boy, unconscious but still clinging to the hatch cover, was carried by currents to a beach at the tip of Acklins Island, where a woman — who was his aunt! – happened to find him, almost dead of exhaustion.

We went to bed on the barge. In the morning, bright and early we left for the Turks and Caicos group.

When we got to Providenciales we were told that with our flat bottom and shallow draft we could cut directly across the Caicos bank, thereby saving time and money, both of which were in short supply due to the two wasted weeks in Jacksonville. We decided to go for it. Local knowledge was available but we were too hurried to wait.

And so we steamed out of Provo, taking Leeward-Going-Through-Cut out onto the immensity of the Caicos Bank, 2500 square miles of shallow and even shallower water — a scintillating expanse that might be a magnificent emerald worn on Poseidon's finger.

Beautiful. Magnificent. Unique — and we were stuck on it. As we took counsel in the wheelhouse, we felt the boat bump gently.

"The tide is rising now," I said. "And it is going to be less high every day — the full moon is past."

"It's now or never then," Breeze said. "The sand is soft, the grass slippery…it can't hurt the steel bottom…let's see what these here engines can do!"

There was a likely looking channel several hundred yards to the Southeast. If we could get to it we'd be back in business, …but if we went hard aground with all our momentum driving us on …

"Full speed ahead!" He threw her in forward and gave it the gun. She hit bottom with a shudder but she didn't stop. She shimmied and slewed and slithered — and slowed to a creep — but she kept on moving. A long plume of sand and grass issued from her props, like a jet's contrail. Once, to our agony, she came to a dead cold stop, despite the engines' every effort.

But the tide was still rising and fifteen minutes later she was moving again, the engines bellowing, the noise atrocious, but we were moving. The rising tide saved us. We finally won clear into a lead that carried 6 feet of water, which widened gradually and took us circuitously to Cockburn Harbor in South Caicos via Long Cay to the south.

That night we partied in port and much of the small community of Cockburn Harbor, celebrated with us. We had beaten the bank. Our way home was clear and we didn't dally.

31.

ON SHIPWRECKS AND SAILORS

The news spread through the cruising community like a shock wave generated by a distant tremor, the pulse eventually reaching into every sea and touching every shore — Paul Johnson had lost his boat. On a dark night in late July his 42-foot. gaff ketch, Venus, had struck a reef in the treacherous Torres Strait, taking everything he owned to the bottom. At age 55 he was destitute, and on the beach in Australia.

What made the news reverberate was the sobering thought that if it could happen to Johnson, it could happen to any of us. Ripped open was the comforting veil we cast over other disasters—the idea that somehow we wouldn't make that mistake, our navigation would be better, our boat stronger, our reactions quicker.

Paul Johnson, after all, is one of the sailing world's master mariners, and a charismatic mentor to many cruisers. Born and raised on a Colin Archer, before he was 20 he'd single-handed across the Atlantic in an 18-foot boat. He was cruising the West Indies way back in the early 60's, working as a shipwright or bartender, delivering sinking schooners and detonating underwater wrecks. Selling the 18-footer to a museum, he built little Venus, a 28-foot double-ended gaff ketch. She took Paul on numerous trips back and forth across the Atlantic, spending winters in St. Barts and summers in England, frequenting the Azores, the Canaries, and the Bahamas en route.

I first met him in 1972 when I woke up and found little Venus anchored next to me. Paul had blithely sailed her between rocks and shoals into Gustavia's crowded teacup harbor on a dark squally night — with no chart and no engine.

There he was famous for drinking rum late into the night yet rising every dawn to work — when he was working. He built a 34-foot Venus for a friend in 6 months, to get it over with, he said, so he could get back to painting and sailing. He subsisted on little money — the sea, art, love, and friends were free and in the West Indies rum was cheap. He was fond of boasting, with a roar of laughter shaking his bearded, weathered face, that he'd always lived far beyond his means.

Big Venus was built in the mid-seventies in Bermuda and — typically — when Paul sailed off, ten more of his designs were being constructed on that little island by people who'd caught the spark.

His 42-footer combined sweet and salty lines with immense room and strength, a boat to weather a hurricane or raise a family, haul a cargo or cruise comfortably around the world. Proponents of fin keel go-fasts called it under canvassed and overbuilt, suggesting that Paul must have been terrified by the sea. He was quick to agree, with stories of being pitch-poled in the North Sea winter in his 18-footer. Enough have shared his fears to build over a hundred of his designs in backyards and boatyards worldwide.

Seeing the likes of Paul Johnson, or Moitessier, or Slocum shipwrecked is, on the one hand, scary, but on the other hand it's kind of reassuring. Obviously, time and fortune have their way with everyone. If you venture, at some point you may well lose; but if you do, don't fret — you're in good company. Poseidon issues writs of safe conduct to no one. Prepare your ass off; disaster can still sneak up from behind, when you least expect it. You can cross oceans and weather gales with impunity, then brush up against death on a riverbank. Choose the ideal season and route for a passage, and still run smack into a fluke hurricane. Some sailors put their faith in high-tech gear, or in meticulous preparation, but at bottom safety is also a matter of luck.

Take Venus, for instance. She was a simple vessel, devoid of many modern "essentials." Paul's electronics consisted of a battery, a solar panel, and a tape deck, yet he rode in safety through storms that sank ships that could pinpoint within yards precisely where they were sinking. Conversely, a "state of the art" yacht lies on a remote reef north of Venezuela. Her gel-coat still reflects the sun for miles off, but up close one sees where salvagers used a chainsaw to rip out her banks of instruments. No expense had been spared outfitting that yacht, yet she ended up on a reef too. Her time had come. Boats, like their owners, all die, and none can predict when.

I remember preparing for our first offshore voyage years ago with the idea that every eventuality could and should be foreseen. After months of reading and buying and organizing, running out of money and patience, we traded in the fantasy of the perfect boat and simply sailed off in the best we had. Now I sometimes feel most vulnerable when I've most got it together. Life isn't safe — it's not meant to be. You just have to trust your luck and play the cards you're dealt.

There's the fascination of the sea — no guarantees, notwithstanding one's wealth, work or good intentions. It's infinitely bigger than we are. Hardships and setbacks are integral to its experience.

When worse comes to worst, being shipwrecked builds character. We all admire the survivor of an ordeal, the extreme testing of one's personal resources — and we suspect that such intensity confers a deeper awareness, of self and the sea, than is known by less eventful lives.

So it goes, on land and sea, that all of life's wrecks force us to drag deep on the cup of knowledge and swallow its bitter but potent dregs. If the ocean held no reefs or squalls, if no ships sank and no one ever drowned, who would ever bother to go to sea?

32.

FACE TO FACE AT OCEAN BIGHT

Just before midnight on July 3, 2001 my boat, my hand-built home, slammed into the low rocky shore of Great Inagua with the momentum of a runaway freight. After 32 years of cruising and a hundred thousand miles under the keel my luck had finally run out.

I was asleep down below, believing the boat to be clearing the nearest land by at least six miles, when simultaneously a dreadful thump and a sickening crack electrified me in my bunk. For a timeless instant I prayed that it was a container, a submarine…or a nightmare.

But then she struck again, keel on bedrock in four-foot seas, and all doubt and hope vanished She bucked and thudded up an incline, then slewed violently to port, and came to a halt canted far over on her starboard side. She lay there shuddering as each wave struck her flank.

I climbed out the companionway and looked about — the boat was jammed up against a ledge of dark coral rock that came two feet out of the sea and stretched uniformly in both directions as far as the night would let me see.

Land, deadly land …what had I done? The noise was awful — the sails maniacally flogging, rank after rank of breakers exploding, seething up and down against the endless phalanx of carved points and blades that guarded this coast. Watching it I felt like a block of cheese eyeing a grater.

We all got ashore easily though, clinging to the main boom, whose end hung over dry land. We brought off the basics and some bedding, then tried to get some sleep, but the rudder kept me awake — every sea slammed it back and forth with a snap that sounded like rifle shot. I left my wife's side after she drifted off and sat looking at my vessel in numb disbelief.

Breath wasn't just another boat to me. I'd built her with my own two hands — the biggest accomplishment of my life. She was my career, and then some. I chartered her to make a living, cruised on her to find life's meaning, and sailed on her just for fun.

My 89-year-old dad, who had taught me how to sail, hugged me for a long, wordless moment "I'm so sorry, son," he said. He had called me up a couple of months ago and asked, "Got room for an old salt? ... One last trip." The grand old man.... he'd been saying that since he was 77, when he sailed with us from St. John to Portugal.

I agonized at the thought of telling our two sons who were so proud of Breath, their childhood home. She had borne our family safely all over the Caribbean, twice across the Atlantic, and explored the Mediterranean, Africa, North and South America. Breath was a part of who we were.

And on St. John, Breath was the largest boat built there in living memory. People loved watching her sail to her mooring under her traditional gaff rig, often to the accompaniment of a long melodious blast on a conch horn somewhere in the hills.

I had let everybody down — and I didn't even know how.

Finally I dozed, and dreamed that my boat was a horse with a broken leg and a pistol was in my hand and I wasn't sure who to shoot — the horse, or myself.

None of our distress calls on VHF had been answered so Mishka, 25, youngest and strongest, volunteered to go for help. He strode off not long after sunrise, carrying a hat, an extra pair of shoes and only one gallon of water. He didn't want the weight of a second gallon in his pack. He planned to move fast.

Steve and I were lashing a sail to a driftwood frame when

I thought to bring the VHF and battery ashore to the low ridge behind our camp, the highest ground around. Within 15 minutes we raised the "Bahamas", which raced to our rescue.

The ship was immaculate, and its personnel showed us the utmost kindness. The cook made us lunch and the medical officer gave dad a check-up and patched up Dorothy's hand. As we sped away I caught a last glimpse of my boat. Realistically, I knew my chances of sailing her again were as remote as the coast she lay upon.

Mishka ran under the blazing sun. For a NYC writer/musician he was getting a jolt of raw reality. Either he had overestimated what his speed would be or we had misjudged the distance. He'd finished the last of the water an hour ago; for the first time it occurred to him, with a spike of fear, that he could die out here...

He found a puddle of muddy liquid and filtered this through his shirt and drank it. Eventually he started to hallucinate...boats, people calling. Desperate, he captured his own urine and gulped it down, then stumbled on, telling himself over and over that my dad's life depended on him. It was sheer luck that a turtle research boat went far up the coast that day and found him staggering on the verge of collapse. Even so he had covered a distance the Inaguans marveled at.

He was at the dock waiting for us cheerily, betraying not a trace of his ordeal, when we arrived.

Hope springs eternal and in sleepy Matthewtown I immediately pursued a salvage attempt — but the local boats were all too small to pull her off. The only vessel big enough was a battered coastal trader anchored in the roadstead but her captain, who agreed to try, kept coming up with excuses and the weather, a steady thirty knots every day, made it risky. Influential friends in St. John tried through contacts in DC to get the US Coast Guard to help, but the CG mission was to save lives, not property — and I couldn't get through to them that Breath was my life. The nearest salvage company, in the Turks and Caicos Islands didn't answer its phone, and local knowledge doubted its boat could do it. I even tried asking the Bahamas, but the captain declined to risk his nation's flagship on a bottomless lee shore.

Each possibility had brought a surge of hope and then a crash. As Steve said, we were riding an emotional roller coaster.

The only option I hadn't tried was a salvage operator named Marcus Mitchell. He lived 300 miles away in the central Exumas, had a fine reputation — but I knew I couldn't afford him. Salvage is expensive, and to bring his operation — a small ship, fully equipped with salvage gear and crew — all the way down and back ...we simply didn't have it — not to mention what it would cost to put Breath back together.

We'd just put everything we did have into building a cottage on St. John — Dorothy's long yearned-for house. Also, over recent years I'd devoted more and more time to writing — as yet without much positive impact on our finances. Still, my wife was of that noble disposition that is content to live simply and we'd had a rich life in many ways — you can't have it all.

Dad and Mishka flew out. There was nothing more they could do to help. I urged Steve, a longtime friend from St. John to go too, but he flat out refused. "I'm going to see this through to the end."

In truth the end was looking imminent. Few of the phones on the island worked, except at the small US CG air base where we were starting to wear out our welcome. Walking back and forth to the base to use their phone was time consuming, and often futile. I was sitting in our room at the guest house staring at the walls, wondering where to go from here....when the phone rang in our proprietor's kitchen. It was the first time we'd heard it ring. A knock came on our door "Mr. Peter, you have a phone call!"

It was Terry.

"Peter? Finally! Jug has been automatic dialing nonstop since yesterday and I've been trying all morning! Quick ... Jug has lined up a great salvage outfit in the Exumas ...and.... an anonymous friend has offered to lend you the salvage fee...you just have to say yes."

"Wow...that's incredible ...but..."

"But what?"

"This sounds churlish — but...well, salvage is just the start. You know the expressions: 'Don't throw good money after bad,' or 'don't start what you can't finish?' "

"Don't worry about it," Terry replied ebulliently,

"I'm not worried about it — I simply don't have it"

"You will.... We're going to raise it! St. John isn't going to let Breath die. Cid put a glass jar out at Connections with 'Refloat Breath Fund' on it and people have been stuffing it with money — fifties, hundreds. — We're just getting started.... So, what do you say? Hello? Can you hear me?" The phone was starting to crackle.

"I said YES!"

"Meet Marcus at the airport ... 5 p.m.... make sure you..." The phone almost deafened me with a burst of static, then died.

Excitement rose like a slow dose of adrenaline, but I restrained myself. I had to run it by Dorothy first....would she want to commit to the brutal task of rebuilding the boat? She'd been there, done that the first time we built Breath.. All these years, often seasick, comfort and security a distant second to...to my trip — the boat had always been my trip.

I said as much as we sat on a curb at the deserted Inagua airport watching the speck of a single engine airplane make a long slow circle around the end of the island. "It's your call baby...your turn to drive our life."

She sat with her eyes closed, thinking for quite awhile and finally said, "We can't just leave her there — without trying our utmost to save her. She is such a good boat, never let us down — she's where we raised our boys....she's our family home!" Tears suddenly welled up in her eyes and I hugged her close — my dear wife, staunch in adversity, with a spirit like a spotlight.

Marcus Mitchell's card listed him as CEO but he moved more like a cheetah — grace, with underlying power. He'd circled Breath twice in his single engine plane and was pretty sure he could get her off, but a lot would depend on wind and sea.

"I like your boat — incredibly strong to still be intact.

Most boats would have been a pile of fiberglass shards by now. Since you're uninsured I'll knock off —%. I'll mostly be covering my costs."

"Thanks — but you'll also have to do it on faith. All I've got to give you is a grand. My friends will be sending money to your account in Lauderdale. That OK?" He nodded, we shook hands and he took off. We'd meet them in 36 hours.

When we got back to the wreck site — a story in itself — Breath, was looking just as we had left her — until we went inside. At high tide seawater was up well over the engine. The bulkhead in the head was fractured, a big coral rock three feet in diameter protruded through the hull. The movement of the boat set waves of flotsam in motion — books, matches, clothes, bottles, toothbrush a stupefying collection of what was now trash.

The salvors arrived at dawn in their vessel the 105-foot Victoria. By midday, Marcus and his partner "Croc" had proved to be masters at their work.

They packed the boat's interior with truck tire inner tubes, inflated them, and passed a nylon lifting strap through the propeller aperture and rigged it to a bridle and 400 feet of towing hawser. Then with astonishing finesse, Croc, at the helm of the Victoria took up the strain and raised Breath up from her death bed, turned her bow towards the sea and eased her back into deep water.

For a moment she looked as though nothing had ever happened, then she started to settle, deeper and deeper, til her deck was awash. There she floated with only her masts and bowsprit showing as they obediently followed the Victoria at speed around the point. It was an eerie sight.

In the calm water behind the point they patched the hull with plywood and underwater epoxy, pumped her out and then towed her for thirty hours up to the Georgetown Marina in Great Exuma who set us up — safe at last — on dry land.

"I'm gonna make money on you," growled Kelley, the big gruff owner of the marina. And he did, but his bark was worse than his bite. He let me leave without the customary deposit. He didn't have much choice — between Steve and us we barely managed to get me a plane ticket to my folks' place in Jacksonville, where I could use a working phone and organize...what...? It remained to be seen. I was flying on faith.

When I arrived and in the months to come... I learned that family and friends are the greatest security this insecure world affords. And that Dorothy and I were blessed with them. How they came through for us was nothing short of fantastic. Spearheaded by three people who gave an inordinate amount of time and energy, the St. John community, those who live here and those who visit, raised enough money to enable us to completely repair and refit the boat.

People gave us a lot more than money... One friend dropped his life, business, everything! for ten days of non-stop phone calls, emails and press releases — a fundraising blitz. Another drove me around for three whirlwind days buying tools and supplies. Another gave me stocks of Burmese teak and African mahogany. Our son sent us a satellite phone so as to keep in touch as the Bahamian out-islands phones were down all that summer. My brothers sent a state of the art full hood, battery–powered respirator. The friend who handled our funds, as if she wasn't busy enough, even organized sending thank you notes on a lovely card made for the occasion.

Things started to turn around fast now that we had the wherewithal to operate. Dorothy and Steve, living in the wreck while I was gone, had become a staple in the diet of the insects from the adjacent swamp, so on my way home from the airport we bought a big fan to keep the bugs off us. That night we all slept like babes.

Early the next morning we got back to work and didn't take a day off for the next seven weeks. We worked dawn to dusk, rising to face a whining cloud of carnivorous vermin and retiring in the same. About the time the bugs quit Steve and I would start sweating like bullocks in the height of the summer heat when all other sensible life panted in the shade. I worked hard, but Steve worked like a man possessed, eager to get the boat to Miami so that he could see his family again.

© Don E. Brown 2004

I tried to get him to go home. He wouldn't hear of it. "I was at the helm, Pete," he'd say with soulful remorse.

"But you were steering the course I gave you, it's my fault," I remonstrated.

"Doesn't matter...I'm not leaving til we get Breath to Florida."

Finally the big day came. Kelley toasted us as we launched the boat. "I have never, ever seen anyone do such a huge repair so well, so cheaply — so fast!" Coming from him it meant a lot. Then we sailed to Miami and five minutes after we tied up Steve was off to the airport to rejoin his family.

Dorothy and I spent the next four months hauled out at Consolidated Yachts, on the south fork of the Miami River — the perfect place to renovate a boat. I hadn't seen him in 20 years but Jim Gardiner, Consolidated's CEO, gave me invaluable advice, set us up with his wholesale discounts and stopped by periodically to chat. We did a million jobs, big and little and finally cut the umbilical cord on January 8, 2002 and sailed nonstop to St. John.

Breath performed beautifully in calm weather and stormy. I'll never forget the peaceful smile on my wife's face as she steered through a 40-knot squall, rain hurling down. The boat was truly her trip now, too.

When we arrived I knelt down and kissed the ground of Coral Bay...in lieu of kissing the feet of all who'd helped bring Breath back home.

* * * * * *

"Friends thou hast and their adoption tried,
grapple them to thy soul with hoops of steel."

Wm. Shakespeare

"Mind the rudder or meet the rock."

Cap'n Fatty

Photo by T.A. Carter

About The Author

Peter Muilenburg was born in 1945, grew up in China and the Philippines, went to Dartmouth College in New Hampshire, went to jail in Mississippi, went to ground in the islands, and went to sea whenever he could. He is grateful to his wife, proud of his two sons, and happy in his friends. Find Breath at www.sailbreath.com, and email at breath8@attglobal.net.

Photo by D.E. Brown

About The Artist

Don E. Brown has been photographing and creating images, from all over the world, for over three decades, and has sold his Sea of Dreams® cards, images and posters since the '80s. After 17 years in the Caribbean he presently resides in Annapolis, MD with his wife Pam and daughter Natty. Find him soon at www.SeaofDreams.net.